HOLIDAY COLLECTABLES
A PRICE GUIDE

By Pauline & Dan Campanelli

©1997
L-W BOOKS

ISBN#: 0-89538-092-7

Copyright 1997 by Dan & Pauline Campanelli
L-W Book Sales

All rights reserved. No part of this work may be reproduced or used in any forms or by any means- graphic, electronic, or mechanical, including photocopying or storage and retrieval systems- without written permission from copyright holder.

Published By: L-W Book Sales
                  P.O. Box 69
                  Gas City, IN 46933

Please write for our free catalog.

Table of Contents

Chapter 1: CHRISTMAS — 8.
Cotton batting ornaments, Dresdens, spun glass, cornucopias, scraps, tinsel & scraps, tinsel & glass, glass beads, wire wrapped glass, blown glass, birds, figures, flowers, fruits, acorns & pinecones, horns & bells, fancy shapes, reflectors, kugels, Shiny Brite, Angel hair & icicles, garlands, candle holders, early electric lights, figural bulbs, tree stands, putz fences, putz animals, Barclay skaters, German flat skaters, cardboard houses, bottle brush trees, cards, post cards, lights & stockings, books, toys, cookies & candy molds, candy boxes, candy containers, early Santas & Belsnickles, plastic Santas.

Chapter 2: NEW YEARS DAY — 106.
Tin noisemakers, candy boxes, candy molds, party hats, post cards.

Chapter 3: VALENTINES DAY — 112.
Early hand made valentines, boxed valentines, paper lace, Esther Howland, Whitney, pull-outs, honeycomb tissue, post cards, diecuts, mechanicals.

Chapter 4: ST. PATRICK'S DAY — 130.
Party books, scraps, stickers, cigars, centerpieces, candy containers, candles, post cards.

Chapter 5: EASTER — 140.
Egg dyes, baskets, glass & porcelain eggs, cardboard egg candy containers, bunny candy containers, early German flocked bunnies, American papier mache, other bunnies, celluloid, spun cotton chicks, chickens, candy carts, chocolate molds, Beistle honeycomb, post cards.

Chapter 6: 4TH OF JULY AND OTHER PATRIOTIC HOLIDAYS — 170.
Beistle centerpieces, axes and cherry tree candy containers, George Washington candy containers, commemorative plates, banners, banks, calendars, World War II, 4th of July, 4th of July party decorations.

Chapter 7: HALLOWEEN — 184.
Magazine covers, Jack-o-Lanterns, tin, devils, two-sided, skulls, owls, ghosts, lanterns, pressed cardboard, papier mache, veggie people, witch candy containers, cat candy containers, early glass, plastic, nodders, noisemakers, blowouts, frying-pans, squeakers, tambourines, rattles, horns, cookie & candy molds, toys, festoons, garland, honeycomb, hats & masks, Bogie & party books, post cards.

Chapter 8: THANKSGIVING — 214.
Post cards, candles, turkey candy containers, roast turkey candy containers, papier mache, molds, crepe paper, party cups, diecut cardboard turkeys, honeycomb tissue turkeys.

PRICE GUIDE: — 222.

SPECIAL THANKS TO:

Kimberly Baker

Julia Bartels- *River Run Antiques*

Patrick Lee Campbell

Brenda Smith Chadeayne

Beistle Company

Charles Gottschall

Charmaine Hawes- *New Britain Antiques*

Joe & Sharon Happle- *Sign of the Times*

Rosemary Johnson

Kim Kurki

Joan & Allen Lehner

Pat Molinary

Pat Patrizio

Gail & Jay Reuben

Francine Schmitt- *"Goodie Sakes"*

Jenny Tarrant- *Holly Daze Antiques*

Pete & Delores Thompson

Mary Webber

A NOTE REGARDING PRICES:

This is a price guide, and as such they are not fixed values and should be regarded as reference only. Neither the authors nor publisher can be held responsible for any gains or losses incurred as a result of consulting this guide.

INTRODUCTION

Cold white winter days and long dark nights that twinkle with Christmas lights blossom into spring with baby chicks and Easter bunnies and baskets brimming with chocolate and jelly beans. Hot summer afternoons with "Old Glory" waving and picnics in the park fade all too soon into the shorter days of Autumn with jack-o-lanterns, black cats, and turkeys roasting in the oven. Soon the snow will silently fall and the cycle will begin again, as we celebrate the seasons of our lives with the ornaments and decorations of Holidays past.

Dan and I began collecting holiday decorations almost 30 years ago when we were given a box of antique ornaments that once hung upon my grandparents' Christmas tree. As the years passed we added more and more antique ornaments, gradually replacing all of the reproductions with which we had once decorated our own Christmas tree. Having written several books on the ancient origins of holiday customs and traditions, we soon became interested in other antique holiday collectables as well, particularly Halloween and Valentines Day items. Then, having written *Halloween Collectables* and *Romantic Valentines*, we realized that we were amassing rather large collections of other holidays as well. These we kept stored in antique chests, and annually we unpacked them to decorate our old stone house here at Flying Witch Farm. As the years passed and our collection outgrew the chests and cubboards, Dan built display cases in our TV room, first just for Halloween, and now for our favorite pieces from all the holidays.

Our holiday collectables have given us such great pleasure that we now wish to share that pleasure through the pages of this book. The ornaments and decorations shown in the following chapters date from about the mid-1800's through the 1950's. The number of items representing each holiday are in proportion to the availability and collectability of that holiday, and range from the least expensive to the most desirable. None of the collectables in this book have been shown in our previous books. Each chapter represents a cross section of the holiday under consideration.

In order to represent each holiday more fully, we have called upon our friends and fellow collectors to fill in any gaps in our own collections, and we have had a wonderful time in doing so. In some cases Dan brought his photo equipment to the collector's home or shop- in other cases, they brought their precious treasures here to Flying Witch Farm. Either way, it always turned into a holiday party as we exchanged ideas and admired each others collectables. The result is almost 650 photographs showing over 1100 pieces.

The holidays included here are Christmas, New Years Day, Valentines Day, St. Patrick's

Day, Easter, 4th of July and other patriotic holidays, Halloween, and Thanksgiving.

We have never purchased a holiday item as an investment, but only for the pleasure of admiring it. Still, we are aware of the value of these pieces. The prices given in this price guide do not reflect the highest prices bid at auction, nor the lucky find at a flea market. They represent current prices paid or observed at reasonably priced antique and collectables shops. This price guide is very easy to use. Each photograph is numbered- just look up the number at the back of the book. It must also be said that once something becomes collectable it is also worth reproducing. Even the most knowledgable of dealers and collectors are liable to be fooled by the best of reproductions, and this is not to discredit honest and talented craftspeople who proudly sign and date their work. The only defense against this is knowledge and experience. Observe and handle pieces, and ask questions. If the story sound too good to be true, it probably is.

Some people may wish to specialize in holiday pieces from a specific time period, such as pre-World War II, or holidays of the 1940's and 1950's. This raises the question of dating holiday collectables. Happily, a good number of pieces are marked and these marks can help date these pieces. Those made in Germany from the turn of the last century are simply marked "Germany". Chromolithography from as early as the 1880's may be marked "Printed in Germany". However, in the years prior to World War I, there was an embargo against German products, so a piece marked "Germany" is not likely to have been made in this period. In about 1930, pieces from Japan, Germany, or elsewhere were marked "Made in (country of origin)", up to World War II. From the 1930's on, the U.S. began making papier mache pieces to replace the cut off supply of those cardboard pieces made in Germany. Following the second World War- between 1945 and 1947- pieces from Germany were marked "Made in U.S. Zone Germany", "Made in Western Zone Germany", or "Container Made in Western Zone Germany". Pieces from Japan at this time would be marked "Made in Occupied Japan". After the occupation, pieces were again marked "Made in Japan". Here in the United States following the war, wonderful pieces were beginning to be made in plastic. The plastic of the 1940's is distinguished by being hard, thick, and brittle. By the 1950's, major cities like New York were being divided into mailing areas- the forerunners of zip codes. These show up as single digits between the city and the state in an address, and telephone numbers began with two letters and a number. By the early 1960's, phone numbers were becoming seven digits, and in July of 1963, the U.S Post Office began requiring zip codes. The presence of a zip code does not date a piece to 1963, it means that the item was made at any time after 1963. After 1953, Hong King began exporting to the U.S. and the manufacture of pieces in Hong Kong boomed in the 1970's. In the 1980's, exports from Taiwan became important. After 1976, China began placing a great emphasis on foreign trade, and by the 1980's they were major producers of export items, including holidays.

As we approach the new millenium, we begin to think of time differently. Items from the mid-1800's will soon be from "two centuries ago", a term previously applied to artifacts produced prior to the American Revolution. We suddenly become aware of the awesome responsibility we have to preserve and protect these pieces of holiday celebration for future generations. Here are some simple hints to help the preservation of these holiday collectables. Keep all collectables in a dust-free environment, away from bright or direct sunlight and extremes of temperature and humidity. Things that might be handled, like Valentines, might be kept in plastic bags. Never repair paper with cellophane tape. Instead, use a bit of acid-free paper and white glue. If pieces are framed or mounted, it should be on acid-free matte board.

Finally, regardless of the values of these objects from holidays gone by, their primary purpose was, and still is, to bring joy and beauty into our lives as we mark the changing seasons and celebrate with Holiday Collectables!

> Pauline & Dan Campanelli
> Flying Witch Farm

1.

The annual Christmas tree (#1) at Flying Witch Farm, decorated with antique ornaments.
A cotton batting ornament (#2), "The Heavenly Gates", 12" x 11", was made by hand in the 1880's.

CHRISTMAS

    Glistening snow covered days and fragrant evergreens sparkling with tiny lights- these are the images of Christmas for most of us. Today, Christmas is regarded as the birth of Jesus Christ by Christians throughout the world, but the traditions with which we celebrate this most "collectable" of holidays go back farther than 2,000 years. The practice of decorating evergreens is an ancient and Pagan one. The earliest tree decorations were actual fruits and nuts- hung on trees to magically insure the return of Spring. When Christianity finally embraced the practice, confections were also used as ornaments. Tree decorating was especially popular among Germanic people, who, in later times, produced most of the decorations we collect today. Queen Victoria is usually credited with introducing the Christmas tree to England, but in fact Prince Albert only popularized a custom already known since the end of the 18th Century. In this country the Hessian soldiers are believed to be the first to have had a Christmas tree, but a diary found in Easton, PA contains a reference to a Christmas tree that pre-dates the American Revolution. In the years following our Civil War, Christmas celebrating and decorating became extravagant and ornaments both hand made and commercially produced were available. In little German villages like Lauscha, from the end of the 1800's to World War II, blown glass ornaments were produced in small home workshops. Most were exported to the United States. These ornaments were cherished from year to year and from generation to generation, as is the case with the basis of our collection- a box of my grandparents' ornaments, survivors of a Christmas tree fire.

    Beneath the ornament laden branches of the tree, too, lies a silent world of Christmas collectables: cardboard cottages with snowy roof tops, skaters frozen in their poses on mirror ponds, bottle brush trees and animals of composition, cast metal, and celluloid. And all through the house there are cookie tins and candy boxes, candles, and Christmas cards.

    Images of Santa, the kindly old gentleman, the bringer of toys and gifts, are an important part of Christmas. Santa figures have been made of cardboard, composition, flannel, velvet, tin, and papier mache- and since World War II- plastic.

    All of these wonderful things, the ornaments and candles, the post cards and Santas, all bring joy to the heart of the holiday collector.

                        Merry Christmas!

4.

Ornaments like these from the 1880's were made in America, of cotton batting stitched to cardboard and decorated with chromolithographed scraps or Dresden stars. They are usually quite large, the ornaments on these pages range in size from 10 inches (#3) to 6 inches (#9 and #10). Such ornaments give a tree a distinctive Victorian look.

3.

5.   6.

7.

8.

The stars, moons, sunwheels, and lucky horseshoes seem to be symbols used by magicians, but may be masonic in origin. The cotton batting is sometimes stitched to cardboard printed with advertising of the 1880's.

9.

10.

11.

12.

Cotton ornaments made of batting stitched and glued to cardboard and trimmed with scraps and Dresdens, like the 12 inch Santa (#11) and the 5 inch baby (#13) were also popular in the late 1800's. Below (#14), a silk pansy is attached to a circle of cotton and above (#12), a Santa scrap is glued to a cotton half circle.

13.

14.

15.

Spun cotton ornaments like the 9 inch Santa (#16) and the 5 inch icicle (#18) became popular at the turn of the last century. The wreath below is made of chenile and tinsel rope twisted together. A beautiful scrap (#15) of Santa as a beardless youth adorns this cotton batting stocking shaped ornament. Many of these are German or made of German scraps.

17.

16.

18.

20.

Dresden ornaments such as those on this page were made in the area of Dresden, Germany, in the 1880's and early 1900's, of heavily embossed and gilded cardboard. Some are two-sided, many are not. While many Dresden ornaments were just gilded, some were glazed with brilliant colors like this 6 inch rooster (#19). The others on this page range in size from 3 to 4 1/2 inches. Made in an endless variety of subjects, Dresdens are eagerly sought by collectors.

19.

21.

22.

23.

The ornaments on this page are all made in Germany, of spun glass and Victorian scraps and date to the late 1800's. The "comet" with Santa above (#24) is 9 inches long. The Santa on the spun glass circle (#23) is 6 inches across. Below (#25 & #26) are two sides of the same 3 inch ornament.

24.

25. 26.

27.

28.

Among the most popular of the Victorian Christmas tree ornaments are cornucopias, which were made to hold candy. Some are "home-made", but most were made in Germany, of printed paper, colorful scraps, and tinsel. Those on this page were made in the 1800's and are all about 9 inches in length.

29.

30.

31.

The small candy bucket above (#30) is covered with crepe paper and trimmed with Dresden bands and a Santa scrap. The 10 inch long cone (#31) dates to the 1920's. It still has its original paper lace tucked inside, while one of the two cones below (#32) has had the original paper lace glued to the outside.

32.

33.

Diecuts (pieces of paper cut out or stamped out mechanically) originated in Germany in the 1860's. These were printed in full color separations hand drawn on slabs of limestone, but this process was replaced in 1875 by a photographic process known as rotogravure. The vast majority of printed diecuts known as scraps were printed by this later method, though they are still referred to as chromolithographs, and were printed until W.W. I.

34.

35.

36.

Santa was one of the most popular subjects for scraps, whether they were used to make ornaments with, used as ornaments themselves, or pasted into Victorian scrapbooks. The five Santas above (#36) were probably made to be put on gingerbread cookies. The one inch scraps below (#37) were used on ornaments and the large 11 inch oval (#38) is one of a set of illustrations. Most of these scraps were printed in the 1800's in Germany.

38.

37.

39.

Large Santa scraps like the two on this page, 7 inches wide each, were printed in Germany in the late 1800's to be pasted into scrapbooks or used as ornaments. Today they are framed by collectors. Ornaments like those opposite were made by pasting and stapling scraps and tinsel rope to a cardboard backing. They were produced in Germany, the majority being made between the 1870's and W.W. I. They are 5 and 7 1/2 inches high.

40.

41.

42. 35Y

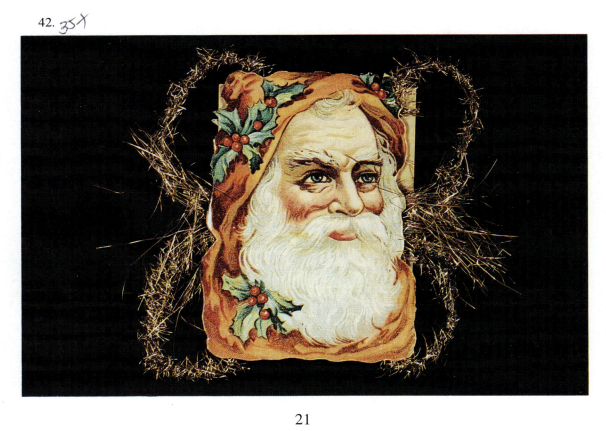

43.

44.

Like the ornaments on the previous page, these were made of printed diecuts and tinsel rope, in Germany, between the 1870's and W.W. I. The ornament below (#45) is unusual in that it is two sided.

45.

46.

47.

Santas are always a popular subject, but those in blue coats, white coats, or any coat other than red are less common and more desirable. The ornaments on these two pages range in size from 12 inches (#50) to 5 inches (#45 and #49).

49.

48.

50.

51.

52.

Like the ornaments on the previous pages, these were made with tinsel rope and scraps. The ornaments on these two pages feature angels, cherubs, and children, and range in size from 5 inches (#57) to 8 inches (#53 and #56).

53.

54.

55.

56.

Angels are usually shown as young women. Boy angels are rare and this one (#55) is especially lovely. The twins (#56) also have a handpainted glass ball. All date to the late 1800's.

57.

58.

59.

60.

Lovely ladies and cherub-like children were among the most popular subjects for tinsel and scrap ornaments. These small scrap ornaments average 3 or 4 inches in size. The largest (#59 and #64) are 8 and 9 inches high.

61.

62.

63.

As with other tinsel and scrap ornaments these range in age from the 1870's to the 1910's, and the clothing on the ladies clearly reflects the fashions of their day.

64.

65.

66.

67.

68.

69.

Tinsel rope was also combined with blown glass balls and other materials in the late 1800's for wonderful effects. Made in Germany, these ornaments incorporate hand painted glass balls, wire wrapped ones, holly berries (made of spun cotton dipped in red paint) with silk leaves, and all combined in various ways. They range in size from 3 inches (#72) to 6 and 8 inches (#68 and #70).

70.

71.

72.

73.

74.

75.

In the late 1800's in Germany, tinsel garland and diecut foil were combined, sometimes with printed scraps to form star shaped ornaments such as those above. At the same time workers in Germany were also tying together stars of crimped wire such as those below (#76), and many other shapes as well.

76.

77.

By the 1890's, ornaments made of a variety of glass beads, strung onto wire and tied into many different shapes, were being produced in Czechoslovakia for an American market. The example at the right (#78) is 8 inches long. In the 1920's - 1930's, similar ornaments (#77 and #79) were being made in Japan.

78.

79.

80.

81.

Simple, early blown glass ornaments were enhanced in the late 1800's by the addition of tinseled wire, crinkled wire, tinsel rope, and colorful printed scraps. The examples shown here were made in Germany.

82.

83.

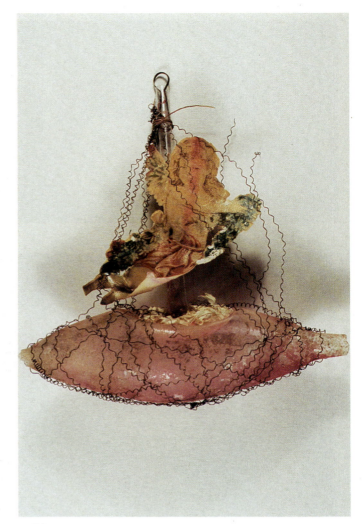

In 1890, F.W. Woolworth brought 200,000 blown glass ornaments to the United States from the city of Lauscha, in Germany. They were a huge success. Glass ornaments blown into molds have been produced ever since, and were made in an amazing variety of shapes, as those below can testify. Lauscha was the main source of blown glass ornaments until W.W.I.

84.

85.

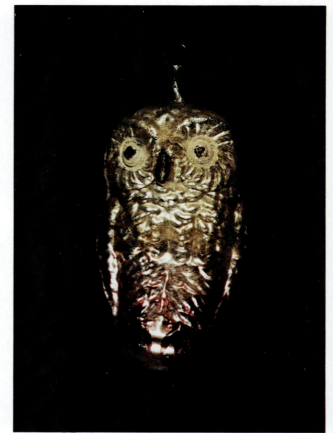

88.

87.

Birds have been among the most popular forms for blown glass ornaments. Since the original purpose in decorating an evergreen in Winter may have been a magical charm to insure the return of Spring, what more natural symbol to use than birds perched in tree branches?

89.

90.

The birds shown here are German, except (#92) which were made in Japan in the 1950's. Most are clip-on (#88 was made both ways) and from their blown glass beaks to the tip of their spun glass tails average up to 6 inches in length.

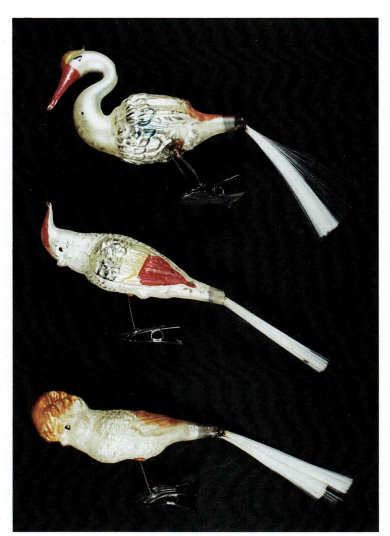

91.

92.

35

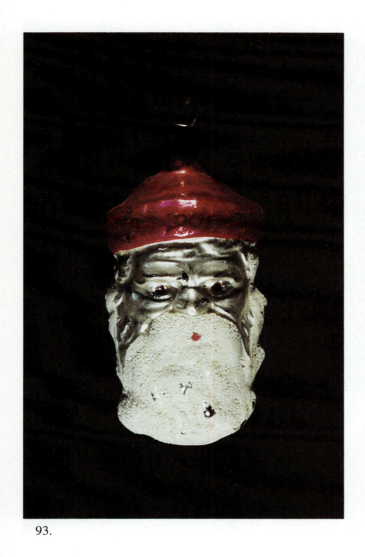

93.

94.

Among the least common of blown glass ornaments are human figures and faces. Santa, of course, is one of the most popular of the human forms. The largest (#99) is 4 inches. The large clip-on Santa (#98) is 5 1/2" high.

95.

96.

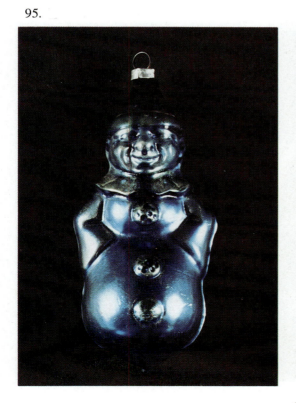

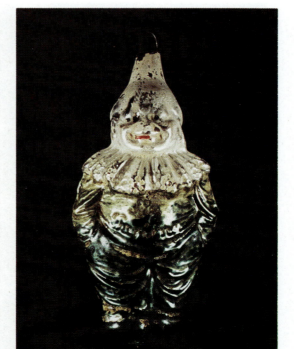

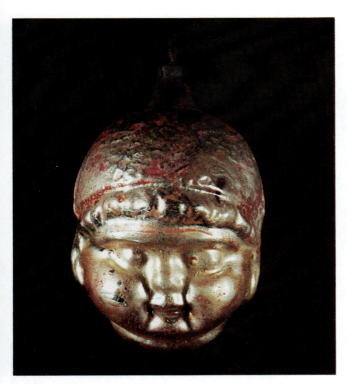

97.

The boy and girl blown glass ornaments (#94 and #97) are both 3 inches high, the clowns (#95 and #96), 4 inches. Forms like these have been made since the 1890's up to W.W. II. Some are now being reproduced.

98.

99.

100.

101.

102.

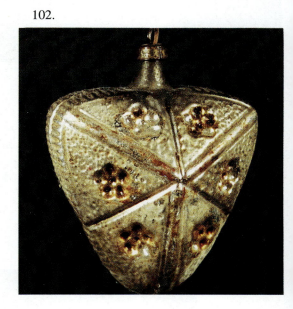

Like birds, blossoms and buds are sure signs of Spring, and they were made into blown glass ornaments in an incredible range of forms and colors, some generic, some botanically correct. Floral shapes were not only made as ornaments, they were also embossed onto other forms, and baskets were sometimes filled with them.

103.

104.

105.

106.

Hearts were another popular motif and were sometimes combined with flowers. The largest among these ornaments are 3 inches high, they are all German and date from the 1890's to W.W. II.

107.

39

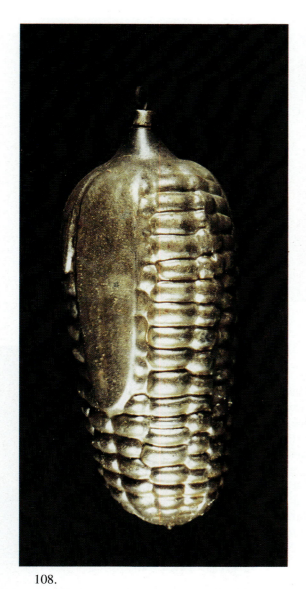
108.

109.

110.

If trees were hung with magic charms to insure the return of Spring, then surely hanging fruits and vegetables on a tree insured a bountiful harvest. In ancient times, real fruit and nuts were hung on trees, but here they are of blown glass, and other materials as well.

111.

112.

113.

These ornaments range in size from a 4 1/2 inch ear of corn (#108) to 1 1/2 inch berries (#112). The fruit basket (#110) is Japanese and is made of composition and glass. The composition fruits (#111) covered with "diamond dust", are each an inch high and are German. "Berries" are believed to be some of the earliest blown glass ornaments, dating to the 1890's.

114.

115.

116.

117.

Like flowers, bunches of grapes were made of blown glass in natural forms like the 3 1/2 inch ornament, left (#115), or merely in symbolic shapes and colors like those above and below (#116, #117, and #118). These ornaments are all German and date from the 1890's to W.W. II.

118.

119.

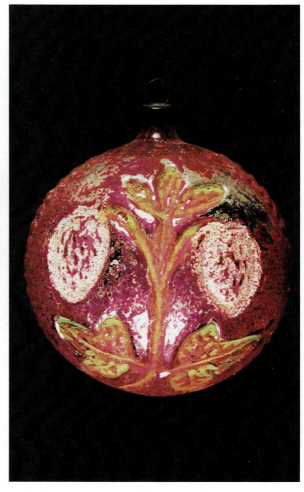

120.

Strawberries seem to lend themselves naturally to being rendered in blown glass. They are associated with May Day in Germany where these were being made, prior to W.W. II. The large red ball with embossed strawberries (#120) is especially unusual.

121.

122.

123.

In ancient times, the oak tree was considered sacred by most of the inhabitants of Europe. Perhaps that is why we still find so many ornaments shaped like acorns and oak leaves. The 4 inch wire wrapped acorn (#123) with silver foil leaves is quite unusual and dates to the early 1900's. Real gilded walnuts were among the earliest Christmas tree decorations, and blown glass walnuts, extremely naturalistic, were very popular since the 1890's.

124.

125.

As the oak was the sacred tree of life to the ancients, so the fir was a tree symbolic of birth and rebirth. There is also a charming folk tale about an elf who rewarded a poor woodsman's wife for keeping her promise by changing ordinary pinecones into silver. No wonder the first blown glass ornament ever made in the 1890's is believed to be a pine cone. Below (#126), a fir tree ornament made to hang the other way becomes a pine cone of sorts. This ornament was also made as a clip-on.

126.

127.

45

128.

129.

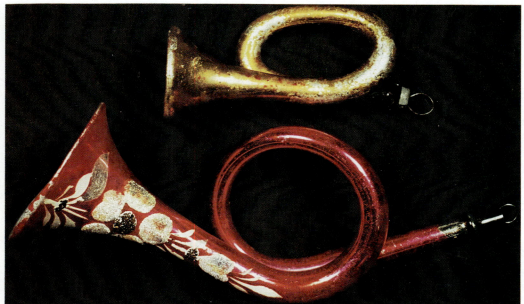

Musical instruments were among the first of the Victorian blown glass ornaments to do something. The eight bells below (#130), up to 4 inches, actually ring with tiny glass clappers- and, as we all know, when we hear a bell ring an angel gets her wings. The French horns (#129), up to 6 inches long, also make a sound when blown. Only the bells above (#128) are silent. All are German and predate the 1940's, except the tiny bells above which date to the 1950's.

130.

131.

132.

133.

As with fruits, nuts and berries were probably hung on trees as charms to insure abundance and fertility. It is likely that every day objects such as those shown here also may have served some magical purpose. An ornament shaped like a purse (#131) may have been a charm for prosperity. Like the French horn, the pipe (#133) also sounds. The charming ornaments on this page range in size from 2 1/2 to 3 1/2 inches. They are German, and date from the 1890's to the 1940's.

134.

135.

136.

As the German glass blower produced ornaments of natural shapes as seen in the world around them, so too did they produce fanciful shapes of grace, beauty, and incredible delicacy. Sometimes, these ornaments are embellished with wires or scraps. The "parasol" (#137) here is 6 1/2 inches long as are the largest of the "rattles" and "spindles" (#135 and #136). They all date to the turn of the last century.

137.

There are innumerable ornaments made prior to W.W. II that can only be described as "fancy shapes". These fanciful shapes are often enhanced with splashes of color or an overall tint. Their endless variations of shape, as well as their availability, make them highly collectable. The ones here on page 49 are all 2 1/2 to 4 inches.

138.

139.

140.

141.

142.

143.

While some ornaments were becoming more complex in shape, as on the previous pages, simple shapes such as these early ovoids (#141), left, were being embellished with bands of design and color. The hand-painted ovoids below (#144) are probably Japanese and date to the 1930's.

144.

145.

146.

Other simple shapes, balls, and ovoids were made with ornamented indentations. Sometimes called "indents", these ornaments with concave areas made to catch and reflect light in new and different ways are also called reflectors. Reflectors sometimes occur in unusual shapes such as in (#142). They may also be embellished with colors and tinsel wire (#145).

147.

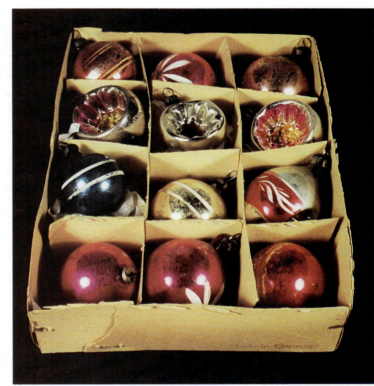
148.

Shiny Brite ornaments such as those below and below opposite were manufactured in the United States since the years just prior to W.W. II. The company was founded by Max Eckhardt, an importer of German ornaments since 1907. Realizing war with Germany was inevitable, he convinced Corning Glass to produce machine made glass balls which he had silvered and hand decorated in his New Jersey plants. Early Shiny Brites can be recognized by their many subtle variations of color. After the war, Shiny Brite became the largest manufacturer of glass ornaments in the world. Those shown here (#149 and #154) date to the 1940's and 1950's.

149.

150.

151.

152.

153.

Kugel is simply a German word for *ball*. Kugels can be recognized for their thickness and weight. Compared to other ornaments they seem able to bounce. They also have flat, embossed caps and the top of the ball is cut flush. Made in Germany as early as the 1820's, they were not imported to the U.S. until the late 1800's. They were also made in New York and New Jersey, and other countries as well. (#150 and #152) are Kugel-like ornaments made in Japan, (#147) is a Kugel-like reflector, and (#153) are true Kugels. These true Kugels are 2 1/2 inches high, and the blue one on the left is not silvered. (#151) is a rare Kugel star, and (#148) is a box or ornaments from Germany with most of the original ornaments still in it, ca. 1930.

154.

155.

156.

157.

Angel Hair, snow, and icicles were all used to give a tree a certain overall appearance. There is a lovely German tale about an elderly woman who couldn't afford to decorate her tree, so during the night a spider spun beautiful webs to decorate it for her. Angel Hair was first used in Germany, but as a garland, not as a web. Here are two sides of a box of Angel Hair (#155 and #156) by the National Tinsel Mfg. Co., showing "great graphics".

158.

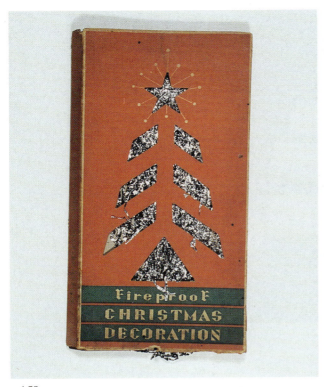

159.

160.

Tinsel was first used in Germany in the 1870's. Packages of tinsel here are made in the USA in the 1930's (#159), and Double Glo tinsel icicles (#160) were made ca. 1940's - 1950's by the Paper Novelty Mfg. Co. of Stamford, CT. "Snow" (#158), was made by the Mica Mountain Mines of Salt Lake City, UT. Here too are icicle ornaments from the 1920's (#157), Diamond Ray Icicles of the 1940's (#161), and "Glo-in-the-dark" icicles of the 1950's (#162).

162.

161.

163.

A finishing touch for some is to drape the tree with garlands or glass beads. Packages of glass beads (#163) in original wrappers, made in Japan in the 1930's came in a variety of colors. Below (#164), simple chains of glass beads combine with handpainted glass in different ways in garlands made in Japan in the 1930's.

Embossed tin clips painted in iridescent colors (#166 and #169) were made in Germany to hold candles on Victorian trees. A clay ball painted gold acted as a counter weight on this Victorian candle holder (#165) patented in 1867 and made in the USA. Brass candle holders marked "Made in Germany" (#168) date to the 1930's, and a miniature Japanese paper lantern (#167) was used as a candle holder on a Christmas tree in the 1890's.

164.

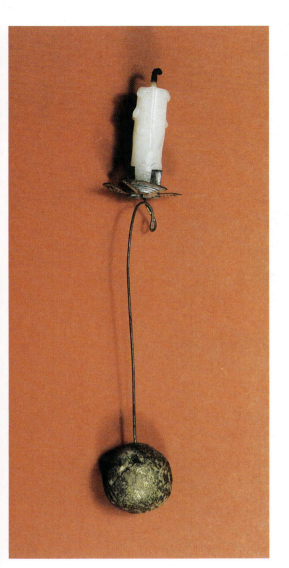

165.

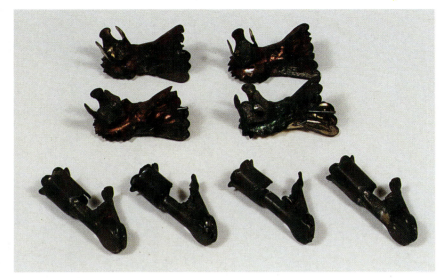

166.

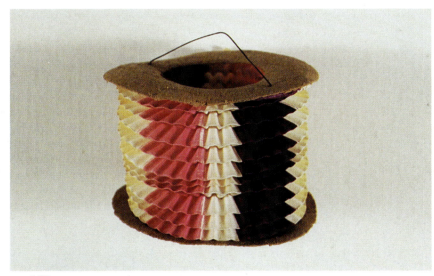

167.

169.

168.

170.

In 1882 the first electric Christmas tree was lit in New York City, with bulbs made by Thomas Edison. Before 1915, General Electric had replaced the carbon filament used in Edison's bulbs with the longer lasting tungsten filament, and created the Mazda Christmas tree lamp. In 1927, fifteen small companies that manufactured Christmas tree light sets (or outfits) all merged to form NOMA (National Outfit Manufacturers Association). Until then, strings of lights were wired in a series, meaning that if one bulb burned out, the whole string went out. Each bulb had to be replaced one at a time to find the one that blew out, but in 1927, "series" wiring was replaced by "parallel" wiring, so that each bulb burned independantly.

171.

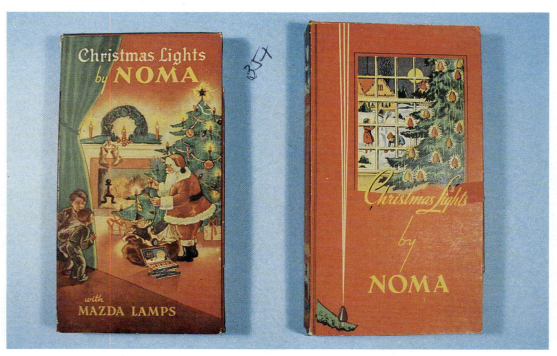

172.

The next significant event in the history of Christmas tree lights was the invention in the late 1930's by Carl Otis, of Bubble-Lites. His invention wasn't released, however, until 1945, after he had joined NOMA. By the mid-1950's they were a huge success, then faded into oblivion. (#171) Two boxes of NOMA 7 light sets with G.E. bulbs. The one on the left, ca. 1930, has cloth covered wires. The box on the right dates to 1939 and has vinyl clad wires. (#170) shows the inside of the box below left, with great graphics. (#172) is a box of Dealites, a set of eight lights wired in series, ca. 1910's-1920's. (#173) is a display box of Bubble Lites, from the late 1940's.

173.

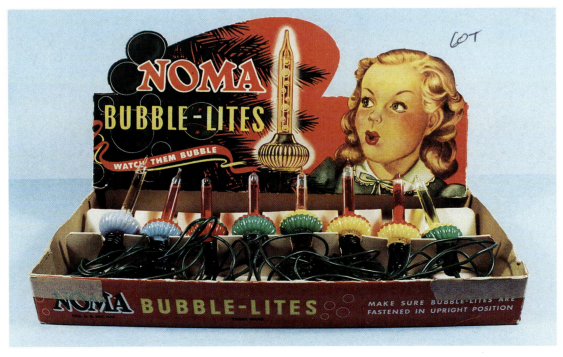

174.

NOMA was not the only manufacturer of Christmas tree light outfits. Here are Reliance lights (#174) in the original box, ca. 1940's, Festive Lites (#175) of the 1950's, and a Timco Lighting Outfit (#178) of the 1940's or 1950's. Even an empty box with great graphics like this one from Good Lites (#177), ca. 1920, is collectable.

175.

176.

177.

Tin relectors, such as (#176), by Diamond Ray ca. 1927, were placed immediately behind the light bulb to reflect and enhance the light. The tiny, transparent lamp shades of Whirl-Glo (#179) by the Sail-Me Co., ca. 1930, slowly spin when placed atop a Christmas tree light bulb. They are each 2 inches tall.

178.

179.

180.

181.

Figural light bulbs were another innovation in Christmas tree lighting that today are extremely collectable. Begun in Austria in 1909, figural bulbs were soon manufactured in the U.S., and by 1919 G.E. was producing machine made bulbs. Prior to W.W. I, Japan also became a producer of figural light bulbs. While the Japanese improved their glass blowing skills, they could not reproduce the quality of Austrian and German paint, so by 1918 they began making figural bulbs of semi-transparent milk glass.

182.

183.

184.

During the 1920's and 1930's, Japan produced millions of figural bulbs including many popular American cartoon characters such as Dick Tracy (#182) and Little Orphan Annie (#185). The Santa, upper right (#180), is by G.E. The clear glass bulbs (#183) are early Japanese and the Japanese lanterns (#181), are classics.

185.

186.

187.
For the collector there are vintage Christmas tree bases to complement the period ornaments. (#187) above is from the late 1950's. The black cast iron with touches of gold (#186) is Victorian, ca. 1890's, and the green and gold cast iron base below dates to the 1920's.

The word *Putz* is Moravian and originally referred to the nativity scene placed beneath the tree, but a Pennsylvania Moravian custom evolved of creating a scene around the nativity that included animals, houses, villages, skaters, circus animals, even waterfalls and fountains with running water. The line between Christmas figure or ordinary gets a bit blurry here. In the following pages we show some more traditional figures. But the Putz scene was often enclosed by a fence, such as those shown opposite. All are hand made, ca. 1910's to 1940's, and are American.

188.

189.

190.

191.

192.

Putz scenes almost alway included a variety of animals, especially deer. Metal deer (#192) made in Germany, are exquisitely detailed and hand painted. They were produced in many sizes and poses. Composition deer such as (#194), also German, are less common but not as desirable as the German metal deer. A variety of birds, including colorful chickens, pheasants, and geese, made of brightly painted composition (#195) are typical Putz figures.

193.

194.

Sheep with stick legs and wrapped with wool or flannel, are also standard Putz figures. Made in Germany, these sheep sometimes bear the word "Germany" on a ribbon around the neck. Sheep, like other Putz figures, came in many sizes. There was little regard for scale in a typical Putz scene, all date from the late 1800's to the 1930's. Celluloid, considered an early form of plastic, invented in 1870 by American John Hyatt, was often used to make Putz animals (#193). It was produced in Germany, Japan, and the U.S., especially in the 1920's and 1930's, and Japan continued its usage into the 1950's. Celluloid animals are usually marked with the country of origin. Some are rattles. They average 3 inches high.

195.

196.

197.

Probably the most popular figures to be used beneath the Christmas tree, aside from the nativity scene, are skaters. Even in a household that has never heard the word Putz, there were often scenes of 3 inch high skaters, frozen in motion on ponds of glass, placed beneath the tree.

198.

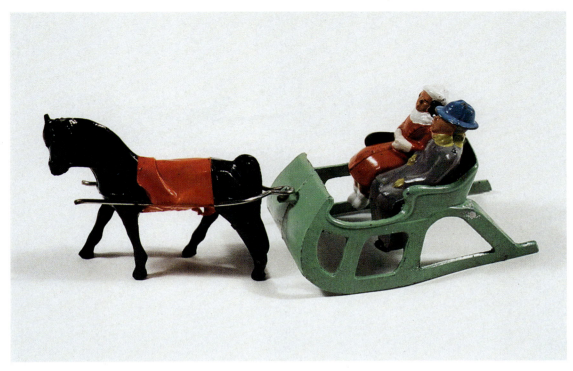

199.

The most popular of these figures were Barclay skaters made in the U.S.A. of hollow cast metal and handpainted. While there appears to be an infinite variety of Barclay skaters, there are actually relatively few different molds, but painted in a wide variety of color combinations. Barclay skaters were produced from the 1930's through the 1950's.

200.

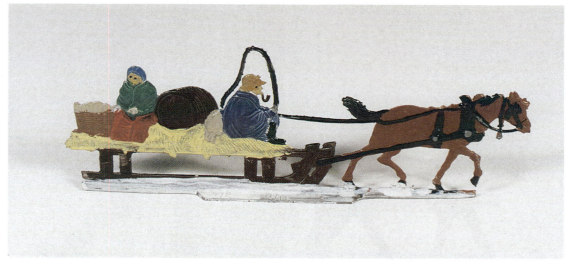

201.

202.

203.

204.

205.

Flat skaters, made by Johann Gottfried Hilpert in Germany in the 1930's, are far less common than the Barclay skaters. There seem to be two sets, one of skaters and one of musicians. Each piece is cast of "white metal", a combination of tin and lead, and is handpainted with the front of the figure on one side, the back on the other. They originally sold in small boxes containing about 25 pieces, 1 1/2 inches high each.

206.

207.

208.

Very heavy cardboard was used in the construction of "Built-Rite" toy houses, which were not made specifically for Christmas, but which have been bought and sold as Christmas collectables nonetheless. Their stunning colors and fine printing seem to recall earlier doll houses by Bliss. At least 10 different buildings (#208, #209, #211, and #212) by Built-Rite average 4 x 5 inches, and date to the mid-1930's.

209.

210.

211.

Compared to the heavy cardboard used in Built-Rite houses, that of which Tiny-Town (#210) was built seems absolutely flimsy. In these 4 x 5 inch examples, red crepe paper has been glued in the windows. The 1897 houses of extremely popular "Pretty Villages" (#213) by McLoughlin Bros., were originally printed in about 18 different styles of buildings, averaging about 8 inches in width. All of these houses were made in America.

212.

213.

214.

215.

216.

217.

Tiny cardboard houses, their roof tops glistening with "diamond dust" snow, are another traditional collectable from the magical world under the Christmas tree. Made in Japan (and rarely in Germany) from the early 1920's well into the 1950's, these charming little houses usually have round holes in the back for tree lights and cellophane or printed transparency windows. (#214 and #217) date to the 1920's, 1930's, and 1940's. (#215 and #216) are from the 1950's as is (#218) which was intended to hang as an ornament. A complete set in the original box (#219) is a rare find. These houses range in size from 2 to 8 inches wide.

219.

218.

220.

221.

To complete the fantasy landscape under the Christmas tree, there are a variety of trees for the holiday collector, the all time most popular being the bottle brush trees (#222 and #225). These were so popular that they are still being made today. First produced about the 1920's in the U.S. and Japan, old ones are still available in sizes that range from about 2 inches to about 2 feet. The old ones have now faded to soft greens and are set in round, square, or thimble shaped bases painted red. Old ones also have "diamond dust" in the snow on their branches.

222.

223.

Other tiny trees are made of bristle and decorated with ornaments (#220) 7 inches high, aluminum foil with cellophane (#221) about 6 inches high. The tinsel tree with crocheted wreath and chenile Santa with celluloid face (#224) is 6 inches high and may be one of a kind. Here also is a bottle brush wreath (#223), 3 inches wide.

224.

225.

77

226.

227.

Sending Christmas cards is nothing new. Here is a sampling of collectable Yuletide greetings. (#226) is a 7 inch pull-down paper lace card that looks just like a valentine. It was printed in Germany, ca. 1900. (#227) is also a Christmas card that looks like a cleverly folded valentine, ca. 1900. It is 3 1/2 inches.

228.

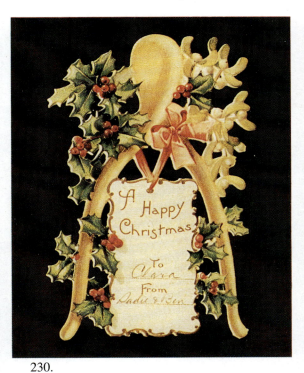

229. 230. 231.

(#228) is a wonderful pop-up card that measures 20 inches across. A cozy room can be seen through the cellophane window. It is Czechoslovakian, and dates to the 1930's. The diecut wishbone card above (#230) is 5 inches high. It is probably German and dates to the late 1800's. The diecut and cleverly folded card with holly below (#233) was "Printed in Germany", ca. 1915, and is 3 x 3 1/2 inches. The cards above (#229 and #231) are light cardboard folders with paper folders inside bearing printed messages. (#229 and #232) have silk tassels, were printed in Germany, and date from 1900-1915. (#234) has a silk ribbon. The average size is 2 x 4 inches.

232. 233. 234.

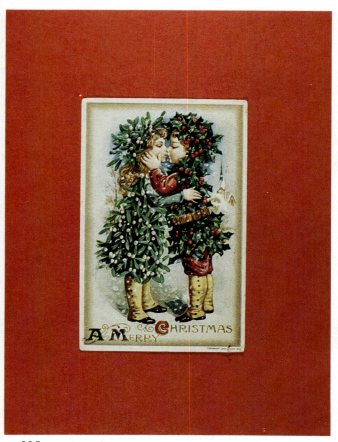

235.

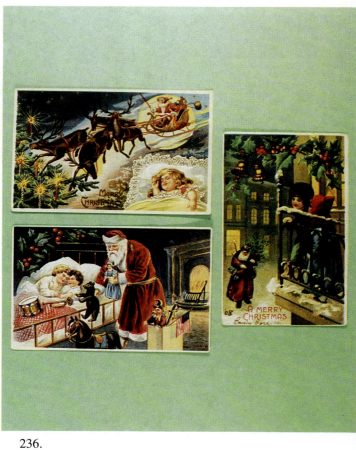

236.

The post card craze began about 1900 and lasted for about 15 years. During this time Raphael Tuck, one of the largest publishers of post cards, organized an international register of post card collectors containing the names and addresses of over 1,000 men and women who wished to exchange cards. Nothing can preserve for us the ideas and traditions of those years as visually and as beautifully as post cards.

237.

238.

239.

Of the many thousands of Christmas post cards that have been printed, those that depict Santa Claus are the most desirable. (#236) shows three post cards by Raphael Tuck. (#235) is a rare card published by John Winsh. (#238) are cards from an early series, as are the two post cards shown in (#239).

240.

241.

Not all Christmas lights were meant to go on a tree. Here are some excellent samples of Christmas lighting all through the house. (#241) is a rare lithographed lampshade, 8 inches high with metal vanes at the top that enable it to rotate from the heat of a light bulb, ca. 1910's. (#242) is a very rare 10 inch milk glass kerosene lamp, ca. 1890, and (#243) is a common but charming electric light, made in Japan, ca. 1950's.

242.

243.

244.

Above is a red cellophane wreath with an electric candle made in the U.S.A. in the 1940's. Below are stockings hung with care in the 1940's (#245) and in the 1950's (#246). The latter still contains all the original toys which were "Made in Japan".

245.

246.

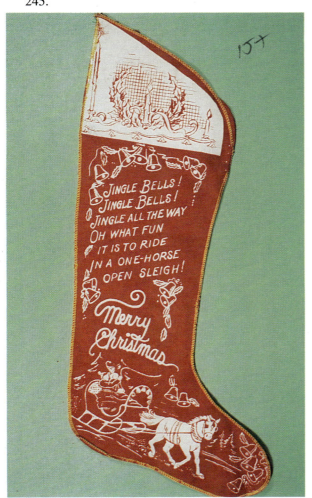

247.

248.

249.

Collectors of children's books as well as holiday collectors can enjoy the titles shown here: (#247) *Father Christmas*, published by Raphael Tuck in 1900 is 14 1/2 x 8 inches. (#248) *The Holly Tree*, by Dickens, ca. 1900, was published by Dutton & Co. It is 4 x 5 1/2 inches. (#249) *Kris Kringle*, was published by the McLoughlin Bros., ca. 1880. It is 10 1/2 x 8 1/2 inches. (#250) *Christmas Cheer*, published by M.A. Donohue & Co., Chicago, ca. 1900, is 9 1/2 x 7 1/2 inches. (#251) *The Bells*, ca. 1881, proves you can't judge a book by its cover. This cheerfully wrapped 6 by 8 1/2 inch volume contains some of Poe's gloomiest writing.

250.

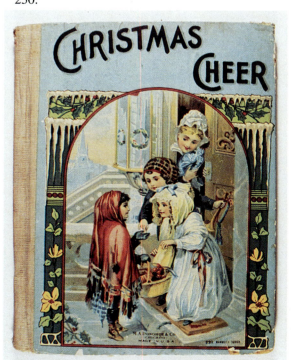

251.

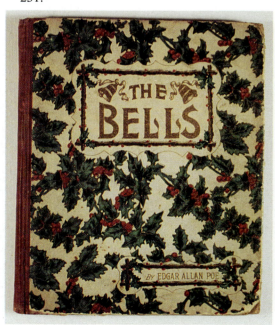

252.

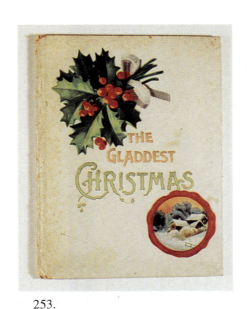
253.

254.

(#252), this volume of *The Night Before Christmas*, is a pop-up and mechanical book. Ca. 1945, it is 7 x 9 inches and belonged to this author as a child. (#253) *The Gladdest Christmas*, ca. 1900, is 5 x 7 inches. (#254) *A Christmas Day*, ca. 1900, 5 x 9 inches, appears to have had the same cover artist as (#253). (#255) *The Night Before Christmas* published by Wm. B. Conkey Co., 1905, is 10 x 7 1/2 inches. (#256) *Santa Claus and His Works*, by T. Nast ca. 1890's, is 10 1/2 x 9 inches. (#257), this edition of *The Night Before Christmas*, published by McLoughlin Bros. in 1895, is 10 x 12 inches and is of linen.

255.

256.

257.

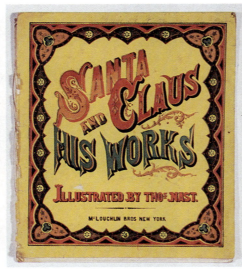

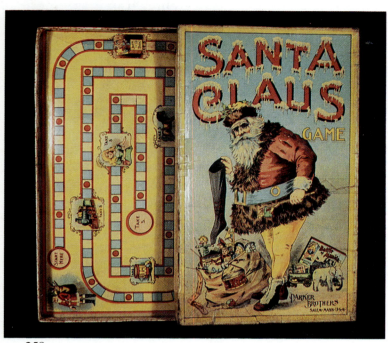

258.

It's child's play! (#258), *The Santa Claus Game* is by Parker Bros. of Salem, MA, ca. 1897. It measures 12 x 15 inches. (#259) the diecut, heavily embossed Santa is German, ca. 1910's or 1920's. It is 15 1/2 inches high. (#260), this diecut Santa with honeycomb tree is by the Beistle Co. of Shippensburg, PA, ca. 1927, and is 11 inches high. (#261), this cast iron Santa and sleigh with two reindeer is by Hubley, ca. 1890's, it is 17 inches long. (#262), this cast iron sleigh by Keyser Rex is extremely rare. It is American, ca. 1910, and is about 18 inches in length. (#263), this tin *Santa Claus Mechanical Toy*, by F. Strauss Corp., dates to 1920. Both the deer and Santa bounce up and down when it is wound.

259.

260.

261.

262.

263.

264.

265.

266.

267.

Baking cookies and making candy are part of the holiday season. Vintage cookie tins, ca. 1940's - 1950's (#266) are a great way to store and serve the traditional family recipes. Why not cut the cookies out with cake cutters like these (#265), ca. 1930. The candy mold (#264) shows Santa riding Halley's Comet, ca. 1910. Other candy molds (#269) are traditional Belsnickle shapes, ca. 1900. Vintage self-wrapped boxes ca. 1940's - 1950's (#268) are a great way to store holiday treasures and they look fabulous under the tree. Stickers from the 1940's (#267) add a vintage touch.

268.

269.

89

270.

Candy boxes like these were made to hang on the tree, or to be handed out, filled with hard candy. They were given by department store Santas or at school or church Christmas parties. The boxes on these two pages average 3 x 4 1/2 x 2 inches in size.

271.

272.

273.

(#272) dates to the 1910's.
(#273) dates to the 1920's.
(#271) both date to the 1930's.
(#270) is from the 1940's.
(#274) and (#275) date to the 1950's.

274.

275.

276.

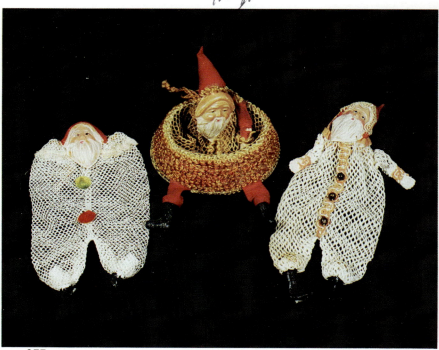

277.

Among the favorite collectables for any holiday are candy containers. Here is a wonderful sampling of Christmas candy containers from years gone by. Santa sits on a stump (#276) that opens just below the middle. He is 4 inches high, German, and dates to the 1910's - 1920's. These three ornaments (#277) with net bodies and celluloid faces were made to contain candy and hang on a tree, ca. 1920's - 1930's. They are Japanese, the tallest of which is 6 inches. The two round boxes (#278) below are made of corrugated cardboard with "diamond dust" snow. Santa is composition, the snowman is cotton. They are probably Japanese, are 2 1/2 inches high and 3 1/2 inches in diameter, and date to the 1930's.

278.

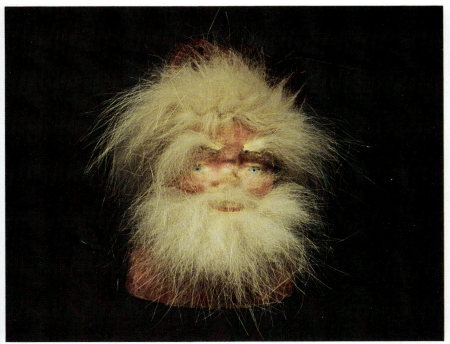

279.

This fuzzy fellow (#279) is 5 inches high and trimmed with rabbit fur. He is probably German and dates to the 1920's. This stork (#280) is a Dresden, being made in Germany of pressed cardboard covered with cotton. One wing lifts to reveal the candy compartment. It is 6 inches high and dates to the 1880's. The three candy containers below (#281) date from 1900 to the 1920's. The two on the left are German, the third is probably Japanese. The tallest is 8 1/2 inches high.

280.

281.

282.

283.

While some Santas are candy containers, some are not. These two Santas (#282) are probably German, ca. 1900 to 1920's. They are 10 inches tall and are candy containers that open at the waist. Santa on a donkey (#283) is a German pull toy, ca. 1900. It is 8 inches wide at the base. The Santas below (#284) are from the 1920's to the 1940's. The one on the bridge is German, the one in front is from Occupied Japan, the other is Japanese. The bridge is 7 inches across.

284.

285.

286.

Blue Belsnickles are rare. This one (#285) is German ca. 1890's and is 8 1/2 inches tall. The group of Belsnickles below (#287) are all German pressed cardboard and date from the 1890's to the 1910's. The tallest is almost 1 foot. The four Santas above (#268) are German and Japanese. The tallest is 7 inches.

287.

288.

289.

290-A.

291.

292.

This gorgeous Santa standing by a tree with a thermometer (#288) may be French in origin. He usually resides in an original wooden shrine-like box with a glass front that gives him a folk art quality. His blue coat and fur hat are rare. He is 18 inches tall overall and dates to the 1890's. The small blue Santa (#289) is just as lovely in his rare blue coat and green hat. He is German, ca.1900 and is 7 inches tall. The deer and sleigh, below (#290 A & B) are one piece, 34 inches long when joined. They were made in "U.S. Zone Germany", 1945-1947. The sleigh is filled with period toys and is trimmed with luffa. The Santa in the boot above (#291) is German ca. 1920-1930 and is 4 1/2 inches high. (#292) is a German Santa in a penny toy ca. 1920's. Together they are 4 1/2 inches long.

290-B.

293.

294.

295.

Here are some more fabulous Santas! (#293) is a very early hollow Belsnickle with teeth that dates to the 1880's. He is 15 inches tall. The chenile Santa (#294), 20 inches tall, is possibly Japanese and dates from the 1910's or 1920's. The German Santa below (#295) with grey trousers and a sleigh full of toys is 10 inches in length overall and dates to the early 1920's. The toys are added and are not included in the value of the piece.

296.

297.

298.

The Santa with the velvet coat (#296) in the original box dates to the late 1920's. He is 12 inches tall. The large wind-up clockwork nodder (#297) is a huge 26 inches tall and dates to about 1900. The three Santas below (#298) are all candy containers and date to 1910 - 1915. The tallest is 12 inches and is clothed in linen. The Santa on the left is French, the others are German.

299.

300.

301.

This gorgeous old Santa (#299) is German and carries a beautiful woven basket of toys. He dates from about 1900 and is 21 inches tall. This Santa (#300) still has his original battery dated 1913. When it is in place the candles on the tree he is carrying would light up. He is 11 inches tall and rare. This beautiful Santa pulling his sleigh full of toys (#301) dates to the 1920's. He is German and the base is 10 inches long.

100

302.

303.

304.

Here is another tall handsome Santa (#302) with an original woven metal basket. He is 22 inches tall and is German. He dates to about 1910. This stunning Santa on a throne of twigs (#303) is 12 inches high, seated, and dates to about the 1920's. He was made in Germany. The sleigh behind this Santa (#304) is actually a candy box. The top of the logs comes off. He wears rare green pants, is German, and dates to the 1920's. The piece is 12 inches long.

305.

306.

Here is a colorful Belsnickle (#305). He is German and dates to the 1930's. He stands 7 inches tall. (#306) is a Japanese Santa made of cloth trimmed with rabbit fur. He is 11 inches tall and dates to the 1920's. The two Santas below (#307) are both "Made in Japan" and date to the 1930's. The Santa on skis is 4 1/2 inches tall, and the Santa with a sack is 5 inches high.

307.

308.

309.

This little Santa (#308) was also made in Japan. He is 3 1/2 inches tall and dates to the 1930's. The handsome Belsnickle at right (#309) is German pressed cardboard. He is 7 inches tall and dates to about 1915. The little Santa and sleigh (#310) are German and date from the 1930's. The deer are recent and have been added for effect. The sleigh is 6 inches long.

310.

311.

312.

By the end of W.W. II, Santas and other Christmas ornaments were being made in the U.S.A. of that wonderful new material PLASTIC! Today they are becoming the hottest new things to collect. These two pages feature Santas made of the hard plastic of the 1940's and 1950's. The Santa on skis (#311), Santa with a sack on his back (#312), and Santa in a sleigh (#313) were all made to be candy containers.

313.

314.

315.

316.

Rudolph (#315) and Santa (#316) were made to be hung as tree ornaments, and this Santa has an opening with a wire spring on his back for attachment to a tree light. The Santa and sleigh below (#317) with the original box was modified from an earlier form to accept the Rudolph figure first produced ca. 1948. The thin plastic (almost celluloid) Santa (#314) was made in Hong Kong in the late 1950's. The average Santa is 4 1/2 inches tall, the sleigh with reindeer is 15 inches long.

317.

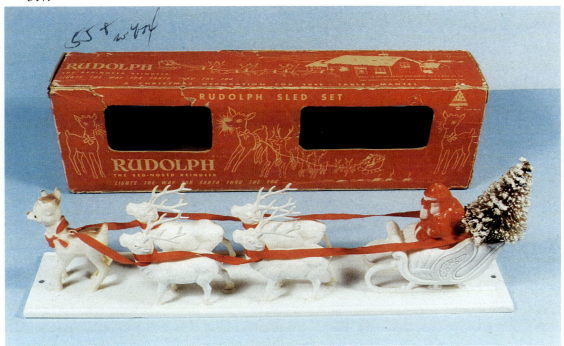

318.

319.

Noisemakers of tin (#318) were produced in the United States from the 1920's into the 1960's by various manufacturers, including: Kirchhof, U.S. Metal Toy Mfg., and T. Cohn. The lovely New Years greeting card (#319), 3 x 4 inches, dates to about 1900.

NEW YEAR'S DAY

In ancient times, the new solar year began at *Yule*, the Winter Solstice, the shortest day of the year. The old year died at sunset and was born again at sunrise the following morning, after which the days began to grow longer again. At this time of the year the Romans celebrated the *Saturnalia*, in honor of Saturn, God of Death, who was always depicted as an old bearded man carrying a scythe. It is this image of Saturn that is still used today as "Father Time", symbol of the old year, just as the infant symbolizes the new year.

In the year 153 B.C.E., the Romans decreed the 1st of January the beginning of the New Year, and we have been celebrating it ever since. In ancient times the forces of death and decay (not evil spirits) were driven out with loud noises at this time of year. Today we collect noisemakers, tin horns, rattles, clangers, and bells made by Kirchhof, Metal Toy Co., T. Cohn, and Chein.

On New Years Eve, we pop open bottles of Champagne. This is not an ancient tradition, as Champagne was only invented in the late 1700's, but it is so much a part of the New Years celebration since Victorian times that noisemakers, candy containers, and even candies were made in the shape of Champagne bottles. Just after the turn of the last century it was a custom to send New Years, as well as Yuletide greetings, usually in the form of a post card.

Party goers in funny hats probably made by the Beistle Co., gather as they have for decades in bars and clubs, in the homes of friends and at Times Square, and await that magical moment, that stroke of midnight that is between yesterday and tomorrow, not the old year nor yet the new. And, when the ball has fallen and the bells are rung, we kiss our loved ones and celebrate a new beginning.

Happy New Year!

320.

321.

The New Years candy boxes (#320) are actually the reverse sides of the Christmas candy boxes (#271 and #272) on page 90. They date to the 1910's - 1930's. New Years Eve and Champagne are inseparable. This Champagne bottle (#321) is actually a noisemaker, a horn made of wood, and is 4 1/2 inches tall. It is dated 1929. The Champagne bottle below (#322) is a chocolate mold made of tin by Anton Reiche of Dresden. It is 6 1/2 inches high and dates from the 1920's.

322.

323.

The party hats on this page (#323 & #324) are probably made by the Beistle Co. of Shippensburg, PA, who produced them in the 1950's, and is still producing them. They are of foil with stenciled "glitter" designs.

324.

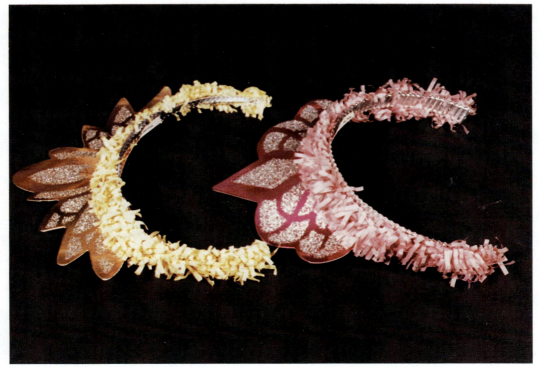

325.

Those who did not send Christmas greetings often sent New Year wishes instead, especially during the "post card craze" of 1900 to 1915. Many of the cards during this period were decorated with the number of the year, as in (#325 & #327). Some cards here (#326) feature elves.

326.

327.

328.

Many New Years post cards bear symbols of the Sun such as four leaf clovers, which are also good luck charms. Others have good luck charms like horseshoes and pigs. As many New Years post cards are decorated with Spring flowers as are decorated with holly or Santa.

329.

330.

331.

332.

(#331) opposite, is a handmade Valentine of real lace and Dresden scraps on a pink felt-like background, probably in its original frame, ca. 1860's - 1880's. It is 9 x 12 inches. (#332) left, is a Victorian heart-shaped candy box covered in red satin and gold braid. It is 9 inches across and dates to 1900.

VALENTINE'S DAY

Valentines Day collectables are, with very little exception, Valentine cards, or "Valentines". When we think of Valentines today, we tend to think of the lovely, lacy creations of Victorian days, but the holiday itself has much more ancient roots. According to legend, Valentines Day is celebrated in honor of St. Valentinus, a Christian who was martyred by Emperor Claudius II for insulting the pagan gods of Rome. It is said that he created the first Valentine when he pricked the message- "Remember me your Valentine"- on the heart-shaped leaf of a violet just before he died on February 14th, 271 C.E., but February 15th had been a holy day in Rome and throughout the ancient world for centuries. *Lupercalia*, as it was called, was a celebration of love and the return of fertility.

The custom of exchanging messages or tokens of love at mid-February is believed to have originated in Italy, and probably had its roots in the earlier Roman celebrations. It survived the plagues and persecutions of the Middle Ages, and by the 14th Century had spread to England. In Europe by the mid-1700's, Valentines were being commercially produced, while in this country they were being handmade.

In Massachusetts, Esther Howland set up her own company with an assembly line of ladies (and at least one gentleman) making cards of paper lace and colorful scraps that have become the very definition of "Victorian Valentine". By the 1860's, Howland is said to have produced 100,000 cards per year. Howland, and former employee George Whitney, continued producing paper lace Valentines and by the turn of the last century, these were joined by fabulous pull-outs printed in Germany. These were followed by gorgeous honeycomb tissue creations made in Germany, and by the Beistle Company of Shippensburg, PA. From 1900 to 1915, post cards joined the celebration, as did diecuts and mechanicals with moving parts. After W.W. I, Valentines became smaller and simpler and by the 1950's, they had degenerated to "cute", but from 1850 to 1950, the golden age of Valentines celebrated the holiday of LOVE.

Happy Valentine's Day!

333.

334.

Here are three early paper lace Valentines in their original gift boxes. The largest (#333) is 9 x 12 inches and probably dates to 1860 - 1870. The smaller, 6 x 9 inch Valentine (#334) was mailed in its original box, ca. 1900, and below, this gorgeous gilded paper lace Valentine (#335) is a permanent part of its beautifully printed gift box, ca. 1880.

335.

336.

337.

The spectacular 8 x 10 inch paper lace Valentine above (#336) is marked on the back with a tiny gold "H", which means that it was made by Esther Howland, ca. 1850's - 1870's. The gorgeous Valentine next to it (#337) is probably a Howland as well, but is not signed. It is also 8 x 10 inches, ca. 1850's - 1870's. Below (#338) is another lovely paper lace Valentine, 8 x 10 inches with its original envelope.

338.

339.

340.

341.

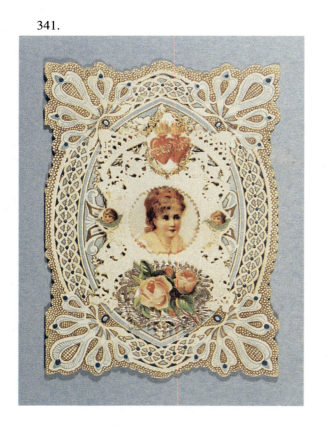

342.

343.

344.

All of the paper lace Valentines on the opposite page date from the mid to late 1800's, and are about 6 x 9 inches. The two above (#343 & #344) have all the qualities of Esther Howland's cards except her signature. They are both about 8 x 10 inches, ca. 1860's - 1870's. Below (#345) are a pair of Valentines with unusual and lovely paper lace. They are both about 6 x 6 inches and date to about 1870.

345.

346.

Here are three later paper lace Valentines. The one above (#346) places more emphasis on the printed scrap than on the paper lace which is one single layer. It is 6 x 6 inches, ca. 1880. Below are two Valentines (#347 & #348) in which the paper lace simply embellishes the printed background. They are both about 8 x 8 inches and date from 1890's to 1910.

Opposite (#349) is a very early handmade Valentine, ca. 1860, with incredibly fine paper lace. It is about 5 x 7 inches. There is no message inside, but a scrap on the front proclaims "Love Me or I Die". The lovely 4 x 6 inch folder (#350) is probably a McLoughlin Bros. and dates to about 1900. The three small, 3 inch folders below (#351, #352, & #353) are all unmarked but appear to be early Whitney made, ca. 1900-1920's.

347.

348.

349.

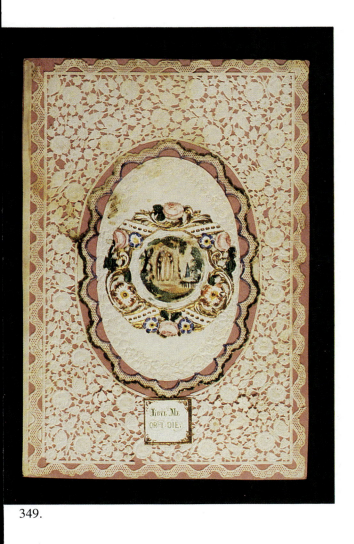

350.

351.

352.

353.

354.

355.

All of the Valentines on these two pages are pull-outs and date from about 1910 to about 1930. They are all composed of three layers that include a diecut background, a diecut central figure in front of that, and a small diecut scrap in front of that. They are all printed in Germany. These range in size from 6 to 8 inches.

356.

357.

358.

(#355) is unusual in having a red cellophane window in the cut out heart in the background. (#358) is unique in having a deep purple honeycomb rosette, and (#359 & #361) are exceptionally diecut and embossed.

359.   360.   361.

362.

363.

The Valentines shown on this page are pull-outs printed in Germany in the 1920's or 1930's. The two below (#364) seem to be a matching pair.

364.

122

365.

The little lady here (#365) warms a heart in an oven in this most unusual 8 inch Valentine. It is a pull-out, but one without a background. Likewise, this 12 inch wide steamship (#366) pull-out appears to be a fully three dimensional Valentine. Both Valentines were probably printed in Germany, ca. 1915.

366.

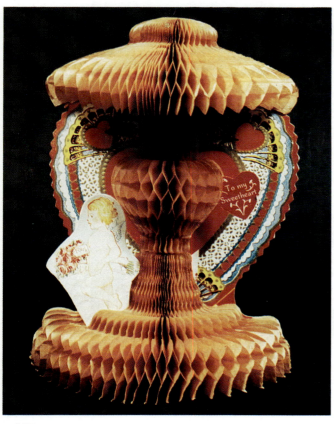

367.

368.

The Valentines on these two pages are all made of meshed, or honeycomb tissue, which first developed in Europe before the turn of the last century. The four Valentines shown here were all made by the Beistle Co. of Shippensburg, PA, which patented a process for the manufacture of honeycomb tissue. By 1925, Beistle began production of Valentines, specializing in "stand-ups" like these, which open to half-round and have easel backs. They average 6 by 8 inches.

369.

370.

371.

372.

The two charming Valentines above are both made in Germany where honeycomb was made with finer smaller cells. The small, 3 inch high white one (#371) is dated 1915. The rose basket (#372) has a separate embossed cardboard heart attached to it by a fine gold wire. It is about 6 inches high. The elegant limousine (#373) has a honeycomb tissue roof and hood. It is 12 inches long and dates to the 1920's.

373.

374.

375.

376.

Some of the easiest Valentines to collect are the post cards, which in many cases are as lovely and as flowery as more costly Valentines. Most Valentine post cards date to the period of the "post card craze" ca. 1900-1915, but the embossed plastic post card (#375) was sent to Dan's mother by his father in the 1950's. The five cards below (#376) are a series.

377.

Post cards are usually embossed to enhance the printing, but the three post cards below (#379) are very heavily embossed, and glazed. The two cards right (#378) are beautiful examples of "Art Nouveau".

378.

379.

380.

381.

382.

The tiny diecuts shown on this page are some of the earlier, lovelier ones. They are simply cut-outs, with simple messages printed on them. These are probably all German and date to the 1910's or 1920's. They average 3 inches high. Later diecuts degenerated to the artless sheets of popouts of the 1940's and 1950's made for school children.

383.

384.

385.

386.

387.

As opposed to simple diecuts, mechanicals DO something. Here, a tiny violinist (#386) may slide his bow across the strings; a goose (#387) reaches up to frighten a kitten; a young man (#388) changes scenes on a stage when a wheel behind the card is turned; and a puppy (#389) rolls his eyes when his paw is lifted. They are probably all German and date to the 1920's-1930's. They average 3 to 5 inches high.

388.

389.

ST. PATRICK'S DAY

The green and white effect of the St. Patrick's Design of the Perkins Ornamental Crepe Paper and Emerald Green Perkins Velvo Crepe Paper is very pleasing. The dancing figures in the center are cut from the Perkins Ornamental Crepe Paper, mounted on cardboard and stood up. The nut cups, shamrock ruffles for the center strips of decorations, and shamrocks on plates and tablecloths all come from the St. Patrick's Design of Perkins Ornamental Crepe Paper.

LASSIE COSTUME

A full skirt of green tarlatan or cambric is covered with a series of ruffles, scalloped in the form of shamrocks, and gathered onto a waistband. A plain White Perkins Velvo waist has full puffed sleeves tied in with green ribbon or Crepe Paper. The bodice is cut from cardboard and covered with Jade Green Perkins Velvo Crepe Paper. The shoulder straps are Green Paper over strips of cloth fastened onto the bodice with adhesive tape. A full White Perkins Velvo cap is fluted around the edge and has shamrocks around the gathering.

LADDIE COSTUME

Make knee length, tight fitting trousers of Emerald Green Perkins Velvo Crepe Paper. Sew them onto a cambric waist and attach a Black Perkins Velvo Crepe Paper vest which has been edged in Yellow. The cut-a-way coat is made of green with a high collar and Goldenrod frogs. Black Perkins Velvo Crepe Paper cut in strips four inches wide are wound around the legs. The black tie is tied around the outside of the collar. Either a small felt hat of black or a plain one of Black Crepe Paper crushed into shape may be used.

Instructions for a St. Patrick's Day party are given in this 5 x 7 inch Festival Book (#390), by American Tissue Mills of Holyoak, MA, printed in 1930.

This potato (#391) with embossed shamrock is actually a candy container made in "Germany", ca. 1920's-1930's.

391.

ST. PATRICK'S DAY

St. Patrick's Day, a religious holiday in Ireland, was first celebrated in America in 1737. Originally, the holiday commemorated the death of Ireland's patron saint on March 17, 493 C.E., but today it is a celebration of Ireland itself. It is a day for the "wearing of the green", the color of nature after her long Winters nap, as well as the color of the "Emerald Isle", and a time when everything from carnations to mashed potatoes and beer, to the line down 5th Ave. in New York City, are colored green.

And, of course, green is the predominant color of most St. Patrick's Day collectables. Some of the earliest of these are the composition or plaster candy containers made in Germany from about 1910 through the 1930's. There are also German candy containers made of pressed cardboard. In this country, Dennison produced stickers, crepe papers, and cardboard cut-outs, while Beistle manufactured cardboard party hats and honeycomb tissue centerpieces. Beginning in 1921, St. Patrick's Day was the first ethnic holiday for which the Beistle Co. made party items. One of these was a hat adorned with shamrocks and an Irish harp.

Later, the Japanese joined in with charming little crepe paper and spun cotton decorations, while crepe paper items made in the U.S. were embellished with diecuts printed in Germany. Along with the traditional Irish harp, such good luck symbols as the four leaf clover and the horseshoe also adorn St. Paddy's Day decorations, probably referring to the luck of the Irish.

When the Ides of March have passed and the onions have been planted, it is time to salute our Irish neighbors, and those who wish they were, with a hearty Happy St. Patrick's Day!

Erin Go Bragh!

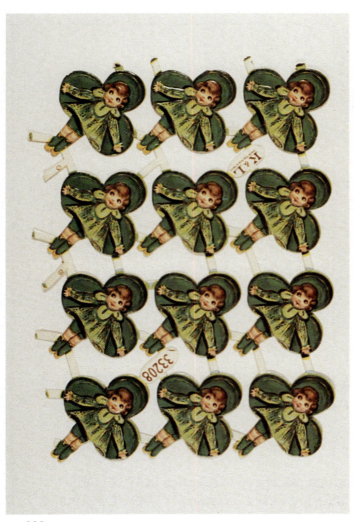

392.

393.

These German diecut scraps (#392 & #394) and this box of stickers (#393) by Dennisons, ca. 1920's-1930's, could all be used for do-it-yourself party decorations.

394.

395.

These cigar boxes (#395) with graphics of Ireland, must have been favorites for St. Paddy's Day, ca. 1940's - 1950's.

The fan (#396) folds up neatly into a cigar. It is 12 inches open, ca. 1930's. It was made in Japan.

The crepe paper centerpiece below (#397) was also made in Japan in the mid to late 1950's. It is 12 inches wide.

396.

397.

398.

The little cardboard box (#398), wrapped in green crepe paper and decorated with miniature shamrocks, pipe, etc. is a chocolate wafer box, ca. 1920's-1930's. It is 2 x 2 1/2 inches. The leprechaun below (#399) stands on a candy box and was made in Germany in the 1920's-1930's. He is 4 inches high. The pair of 9 inch candles (#400) were made for St. Paddy's Day celebration. The back of the lasses dress is covered with shamrocks, ca. 1940's-1950's. Paddy's Pig (#401) is of green flocking and is a candy container, 5 1/2 inches long, ca. 1920's-1930's. It was made in Germany as was the Irish gentleman candy container below (#403). Just the skin of a rabbit fur mustache remains on this rare Irish gentleman nodder (#402). He is 5 inches tall and was made in Germany, ca. 1930's.

399.

400.

134

401.

402.

403.

404.

405.

The items on this page are all candy containers and date to the 1920's-1930's. The hat (#405) was made in Japan. The little laddie, left (#404), is beautifully glazed composition and was made in Germany, as were the lovely lasses below. All are 3 to 4 1/2 inches tall.

406.

407.

The Irish gentleman and gentry below (#408) are also candy containers, made in Germany in the 1920's and 1930's. They are 3 to 4 inches tall. The post card above (#407) with a green tin horseshoe was a St. Patrick's Day greeting, and was posted in its own gift box in the 1920's.

408.

409.

410.

411.

412.

413.

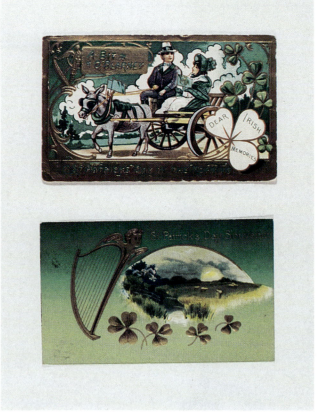

414.

As with post cards printed to celebrate other holidays, St. Paddy's Day post cards date mostly to the period of the "post card craze", ca. 1900-1915. The post card depicting the airship (#409) "Shamrock" is by famous post card artist Ellen Clappsaddle. The pair below that (#411) are exceptionally beautiful. Many St. Patrick's Day post cards show scenes of Ireland and Irish life.

415.

139

416.

417.

This twig Easter basket (#416) is filled with traditional candies and antique Easter decorations. It is American, ca. 1920's, and is 18 inches high.

This packet of Paas Easter egg dye transfers (#417) was made in Germany, ca. 1900. It is 3 x 5 1/2 inches.

EASTER

The first Sunday after the first Full Moon after the Vernal Equinox is the most sacred day in the Christian calendar- Easter Sunday, the resurrection of Jesus. And, for untold centuries before the Christian era, the Vernal Equinox itself promised renewal and rebirth. The name Easter comes from the name of the Anglo-Saxon goddess of Spring, of the East, and of the Sunrise- *Eostre*. Rabbits were sacred to her, especially white ones.

In the countries of Eastern Europe, egg decorating at the time of the Vernal Equinox was an ancient ritual, and the egg is a universal symbol of rebirth. Other symbols of the Easter season are baby animals, chicks, bunnies, and lambs.

It has been said that man first learned to weave baskets by watching birds build nests in which to lay their eggs. Colored eggs and Easter baskets go together naturally, and nothing represents the holiday quite as well as a basket brimming with eggs, chocolate bunnies, and jelly beans.

Easter is the third most collectable holiday after Christmas and Halloween. Among these Easter collectables are German candy containers in the form of bunnies in a wide variety of poses, made of pressed cardboard, composition or plaster, and colorful paper covered cardboard eggs. There are also eggs made of glass, porcelain, and tin. In the U.S., bunnies and other candy containers were made of papier mache, and the Beistle Co. made chicks and bunnies in honeycomb tissue baskets with ingenious clutches of colorful honeycomb eggs called "turnovers". Some of the Beistle honeycomb Easter decorations were made, unchanged, for up to 45 years of production.

Fluffy little chicks of spun cotton or chenile were used to accent Easter baskets, and chickens made of all sorts of materials, including real chicken feathers, were also used to celebrate the season.

So when Winter days have melted into Spring, when the robins have returned and the pussy-willow catkins burst grey and fuzzy from shiny brown buds, its time to color Easter eggs, fill baskets with jelly beans, and celebrate Spring.

Happy Easter!

418.

419.

420.

421.

142

422.

On the opposite page are three Easter baskets made of splint (#418, #420, & #421). They are probably Japanese. Baskets like these have been made in all sizes since the 1940's. One basket here (#419) is made of willow and "moss" (actually luffa). It dates to the 1930's and is 6 inches high. Eggs are traditional symbols of Easter and of rebirth. Here are two milk glass eggs (#422 & #424). The one with the chick hatching out dates to the 1930's, the other dates to about 1900 and was made to hang. They are 3 and 4 inches long. The large egg (#423) is made of porcelain and is hand painted. It dates to about 1910 and is 5 inches high.

423.

424.

143

425.

426.

Cardboard eggs like these have been made since the turn of the last century, and are recently being made again. They are made of pressed cardboard covered on the outside with beautifully printed paper. They are lined inside with delicately printed paper, too. Earlier eggs sometimes have a "Dresden" band around them and inside they are edged with beautifully cut paper lace.

427.

428.

144

429.

430.

Cardboard eggs like these were made to be candy containers. Many cardboard eggs still have a loop of string at the top by which they were meant to be hung. They were made in Germany, and range in size from 6 inches long (#425) to 2 1/2 inches (#429). Most of these date to the 1920's & 1930's, and (#431) dates from the 1950's.

431.

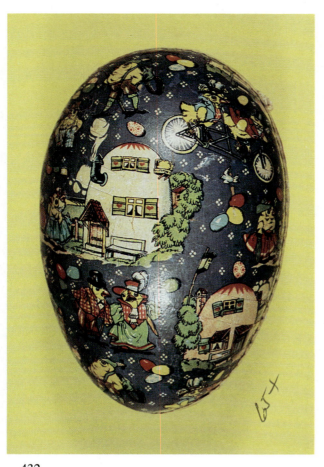

432.

433.

434.

146

The large grey cardboard egg opposite (#432) is 6 inches high and dates to the 1920's. The egg with the bunnies (#433) is marked made in Germany and dates from the 1930's. The three eggs opposite below (#434) date to the 1940's and range from 3 to 4 inches. The large egg in the center is marked "West Germany" and dates to the 1950's.

The eggs below (#436) date to the 1920's and 1930's and range in size from 2 to 6 inches. The large dark egg in the center is from the turn of the last century, and was varnished. The tin egg shaped box, right (#435), is 6 inches long. It once held a chocolate egg and dates to the early 1950's. It was made in England.

435.

436.

437.

438.

439.

Like eggs, bunnies are symbols of Spring, of fertility and of renewal. The two bunnies (#438 & #439) were made in Germany in the 1910's. They are pressed cardboard coated with gesso, and have stick legs. (#438) is 7 inches high, (#439) is 4 inches long.

440.

441.

442.

The two bunnies hatching out of blue eggs (#440 & #442) are made of hollow cast composition and are both candy containers made in Germany in the 1920's and 1930's. They are both about 6 inches high. The white bunny candy containers (#437 & #441) were made of papier mache in the U.S. in the 1940's. They are coated with gesso and airbrushed with pastel colors. (#437) is 8 inches high, (#441) are 7 and 5 1/2 inches.

443.

The bunnies on these two pages are all very natural looking and realistic. They were made in Germany in the 1910's - 1920's of pressed cardboard and composition and have been flocked. Some have glass eyes. The log in (#443) is 6 inches in length, the running rabbit (#444) is 8 1/2 inches long.

444.

445.

The beautiful bunny in the basket (#445) is 4 1/2 inches long. The bunny below with his head tilted back (#446) is another rare pose and the bunny with the carrot is just adorable. They are 3 1/2 and 5 inches long. All are candy containers.

446.

447.

Like the beautiful bunnies on the previous pages, these were made in Germany in the 1910's-1920's. They are of cardboard and composition, and are flocked. Most of these have glass eyes. The three bunnies (#447) range in size from 3 to 7 inches. The large bunny below (#448) is 7 inches long. The two standing bunnies (#449 & #450) are about 10 inches tall, and the little bunny (#451) opposite below is about 6 inches. They are all candy containers.

448.

449.

450.

451.

153

452.

453.

The bunny in the dress here (#452) is a wind-up toy that dances a jig. She was made in Western Zone Germany, ca. 1945-1947, and is 7 1/2 inches tall. The little sitting bunny (#453) is a German candy container, ca. 1920's, and is 5 inches tall. The hen on the nest below (#454) is also a German candy container. It is made of composition and is about 5 inches long, ca. 1920's-1930's.

454.

455.

456.

The rabbit candy container (#455) is made of papier mache. It is American, ca. 1940's-1950's, and is 2 1/2 inches tall. The large rabbit candy container (#456), 9 1/2 inches high, is a kind of papier mache usually called "egg crate", and dates to the 1940's & 1950's- as does the hen on her nest (#457) below, which is 6 inches high. They are both American.

457.

155

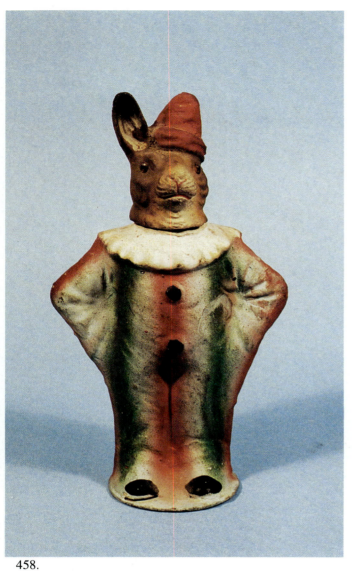

458.

459.

The composition bunny in a clown suit (#458) is a German candy container, ca. 1910's-1920's, and is 7 1/2 inches tall. The rare glass bunny candy container (#459) is 4 inches long and dates to the 1910's-1920's. The brownie riding the bunny candy container (#460) is also rare. It is 4 1/2 inches long, German, and dates to the 1920's.

460.

461.

462.

The two bunnies in their 4 inch high pink house (#461) is a German composition candy container, ca. 1920's-1930's, as is the white 7 inch rabbit wearing a hat and clutching a carrot (#462). Below are an assortment of celluloid Easter toys from the 1930's and 1940's. The tallest is 6 inches high. They are German and American.

463.

464.

465.

Tiny chicks made of spun cotton in a variety of sizes were used as Easter decorations. The chicks above (#464) are about 1 inch high each. The large chick on the 2 1/2 inch chocolate wafer box (#465) is 1 inch high. Two inch high chenile chicks and bunnies like these (#466) were used to decorate Easter baskets.

466.

467.

468.

These 2 1/2 inch spun cotton chicks (#467) have red felt combs and chicken feather wings. The 2 inch chick squeaker (#468) and the 4 inch hatching egg squeaker (#469) were made in Japan, as were most, if not all of the chicks and bunnies on these two pages, from the 1930's to the 1950's.

469.

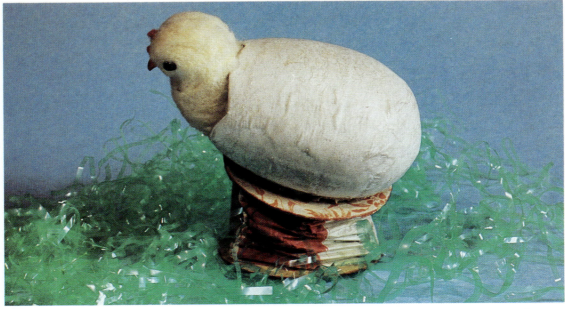

470.

The beautiful cardboard "rockers" (#470) were printed in Germany and were intended to be childrens toys. They date to about the 1910's, and are 4 1/2 inches high. The 4 1/2 x 6 inch Easter egg dye display box (#471) may have held dyes like (#417). It dates to the early 1900's.

471.

472.

This rooster and hen (#472) are both 3 inch candy containers made of composition. They are German, ca. 1920's. The beautiful chicken candy container below (#473) is German, and is of pressed cardboard covered with cotton and feathers, ca. 1920's-1930's. The wing lifts to reveal the candy. It is 4 1/2 inches high.

473.

474.

475.

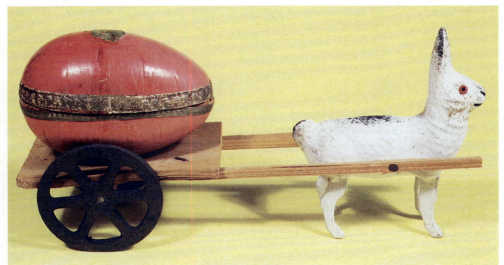

The little moss (luffa) covered cart above (#474) contains a handpainted egg that hides a candy compartment. It is Japanese and dates to the 1930's. It is 6 1/2 inches long. The 6 1/2 inch long cart (#475) is German and dates to the 1900's-1910's. The cardboard egg is a part of the cart and is a candy container. The two cardboard bunnies below (#476) are candy containers. They are probably American and were distributed by Ann-De, ca. 1950's and are 8 1/2 inches high.

476.

477.

478.

The tin rooster pulling an egg-shaped cart (#477) is probably American, ca. 1945, and is 7 inches long. The bunny with the cart (#478) is German pressed cardboard, ca. 1910's-1920's. The twig cart is trimmed with luffa. Today it holds an antique egg but probably once held candy. It is 8 inches long. The cardboard bunny with the cart (#479) was made by the Transogram Co. of New York, ca. 1950's. It is 7 inches long.

479.

480.

481.

Nothing says "Happy Easter" like a chocolate Easter bunny, and the chocolate molds that they were made in are quite collectable. The tin molds shown here average about 5 inches in height or length, the one exception being (#484) which is almost 2 feet tall. The molds on these pages date from the 1910's to the 1950's and were made in the U.S. and in Germany.

482.

483.

484.

485.

The Easter decorations on these two pages are by the Beistle Co. of Shippensburg, PA, and are of printed cardboard and meshed or honeycomb tissue. The Beistle Co., which is still in operation, has been one of the world's leading producers of honeycomb tissue since the early 1900's. Beistle began producing Easter decorations in 1921, and one of the first was this bunny (#486). It is 6 1/2 inches wide and was produced from 1921 until 1966. The bunny in the 9 inch basket (#487) was made from 1929 until 1972. The two 11 inch baskets opposite (#488 & #489) both date to 1925. The honeycomb eggs in the baskets are ingeniously folded "turn overs", and the baskets, eggs and all, fold flat!

486.

487.

488.

489.

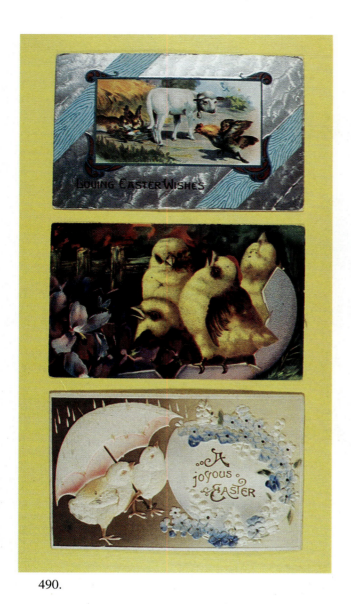

490.

491.

Like post cards sent to celebrate other holidays, Easter post cards usually date to the period of the so called "post card craze", ca. 1900 to 1915. Chicks are popular as post card subjects as are chickens and roosters which are often depicted at sunrise. The three post cards below (#492) are a series and printed in Germany.

492.

168

493.

The carts depicted in the post cards (#494) seem to reflect candy containers shown on pages 162 & 163 in this chapter. The card (#493) showing the lamb helping the bunnies in their love tryst is exceptionally beautiful.

494.

495.

169

496.

497.

This honeycomb tissue centerpiece (#496) made to celebrate Washington's Birthday, was one of many patriotic decorations made by the Beistle Co., ca. 1927-1957. It is 9 inches in diameter.

The little candy box (#497) just 2 1/2 inches across, was made of cardboard and printed satin, ca. 1920's-1930's, for holidays like the 4th of July.

4th OF JULY and other PATRIOTIC HOLIDAYS

The 4th of July, our most patriotic of holidays, commemorates the signing of the Declaration of Independence in Philadelphia on July 4th, 1776. Since the Continental Congress declared the date of July 4th a national holiday (known originally as Independence Day), it has been celebrated with parades, picnics, and fireworks. 4th of July collectables began to be produced in the 19th Century, and especially around the time of the Centennial- 1876. The majority of 4th of July collectables were produced from the turn of the last century into the 1930's. Many of these were candy containers produced here or in Germany, and almost all of these can be recognized by their colors- red, white, and blue.

Almost as popular as the 4th of July was the celebration of Washington's Birthday on February 22. It is said that this holiday was first observed in 1792, in Philadelphia, when a motion was made in Congress to adjourn for 1/2 an hour in honor of the "Father of our Country". One of the traditions of this holiday (until it was combined with Lincoln's Birthday for what is now Presidents Day) was a log cake, or jelly roll covered with chocolate icing and adorned with cherries. This was a reference to the legend of George Washington cutting down his father's cherry tree. When questioned, he confessed because he "couldn't tell a lie". This legend also accounts for a huge number of Washington's Birthday collectables, a wide variety of candy containers in the shape of cherry tree stumps and axes with hollow handles for containing candy.

Aside from George Washington, Abraham Lincoln is probably our most beloved president, and his birthday, February 12th, was also a National holiday. Lincoln's Birthday collectables include commemorative plates and banks.

Other patriotic holidays include Memorial Day and Veteran's Day, and post cards dating from 1900 to 1915 can be found for all of these holidays that are dazzling with their brilliant banners of red, white, and blue!

Have a Glorious 4th!

498.

499.

500.

172

Cut-out cardboard axes like these (#498) were probably made by Dennisons, ca. 1920's-1930's to celebrate Washington's Birthday. They are each about 4 inches long. This cut down cherry tree (#499) is a candy container, made in Germany, ca. 1910-1920's. It is cardboard and composition and is 5 inches high. The two large axes here (#500) are candy containers having hollow handles. They date from the 1930's-1950's. They were made in Japan. The largest is 8 1/2 inches.

The three busts of George Washington (#501 & #502) were all made in Germany between 1910's and 1930's. The differences are remarkable! All three are candy containers and are about 4 1/2 inches tall.

501.

502.

173

503.

This spectacular candy container (#503) commemorates George Washington's crossing of the Delaware to capture the Hessians at Trenton in 1776. It was made in Germany, ca. 1910's-1920's, and is 4 1/2 inches long. The 4 inch cherry tree log below (#504) is a party favor and was made in Japan in the 1950's, but the other two pieces are candy containers and were made in Germany in the 1910's or 1920's. The one on the right is a cardboard tri-cornered hat decorated with a sprig of cherries.

The two figures of George Washington, opposite (#505 & #506), are also candy containers. They were made in Germany ca. 1910's-1920's and are 3 1/2 and 4 1/2 inches high. George Washington on his horse, below (#507) is a 5 inch pull-toy made in Germany, ca. 1920's-1930's.

504.

505.

506.

507.

175

508.

509.

Plates like these (#508) by Royal Doulton of England, ca. 1920's, and (#511) by Johnson Bros., ca. 1920's, were no doubt used to celebrate the birthdays of these two great presidents. This beautiful cake tin (#509) bearing the portrait of Washington, by Gilbert Stewart, may have held the traditional "log" cake, or perhaps a cherry pie. This pressed glass cake platter (#510) embossed with the likeness of the State House in Philadelphia, may have been made for the sesquicentennial, July 4th, 1926.

510.

511.

512.

This banner (#512) was made to celebrate the sesquicentennial of Washington crossing the Delaware, Christmas, 1926. It shows a portion of the painting of Washington's crossing done by German born Philadelphian, Emanuel Leutze, in 1851. It is considered the most important patriotic painting ever done of an American historic event. The glass top hat below (#513) is a bank, and was probably made as a giveaway by the Lincoln Savings Bank. It is 4 1/2 inches high. The beautiful Lincoln calendar (#514) for 1921 is held together with a ribbon and has quotes by Lincoln printed on every page in red, white, and blue. It is 7 x 9 1/2 inches.

514.

513.

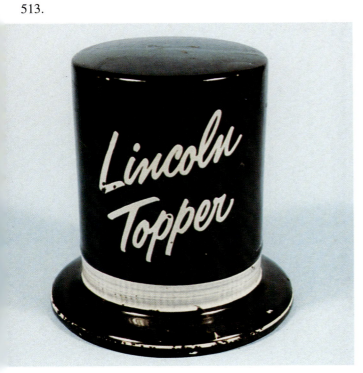

515.

516.

What could be more useful on the 4th of July than a fan? Here are two beauties (#515 & #516). The lovely woman with the staple in her teeth is all American and dates to the early 1940's. The cigar, given out to celebrate the birth of the nation, opens into a fan 10 inches long. It is Japanese and may date to the 1930's. The patriot crayons (#517) dates to the turn of the last century. Photos A & B show both sides of the box.

517-A.

517-B.

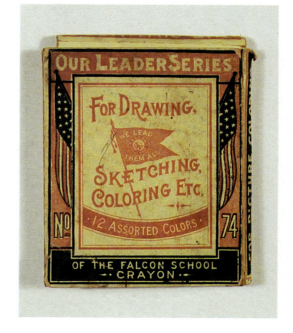

518.

519.

Sparklers are a traditional part of a 4th of July celebration and these (#518), ca. 1940's, are decorated for the holiday. The Victory Doll (#519) is dressed for any patriotic holiday. She is 6 1/2 inches tall and dates to the early 1940's. A ribbon across her chest proclaims "Bundles for America". The 4 inch Uncle Sam pipe (#520) was made in Japan in the 1950's and the slate pencils date to about 1900.

520.

179

521.

522.

523.

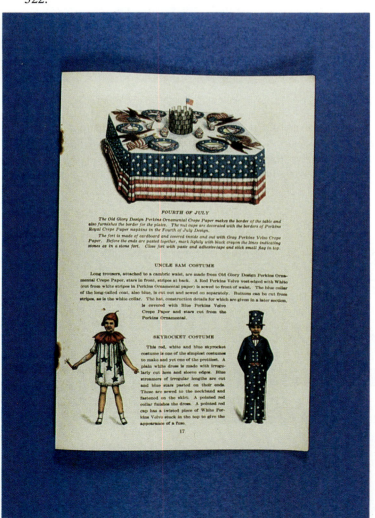

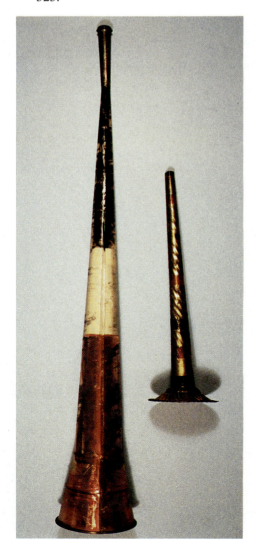

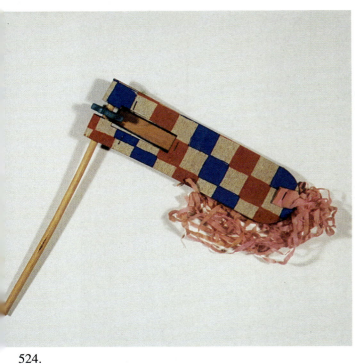

524.

525.

Here is everything necessary for a 4th of July or patriotic party, even instructions (#522), from the Festival book by American Tissue Mills, Holyoak, MA, ca. 1930. Nut cups (#521) in patriotic colors are probably by C.A. Reed, ca. 1940's. Noisemakers include tin horns (#523), ca. 1910 and 1926, up to 2 feet long, and a cardboard ratchet (#524). Paper napkins like this one (#525) and crepe paper (#526), probably by Dennison, dates to the 1910's-1930's. The honeycomb tissue garland is probably by Beistle. It opens to about 10 feet and dates to around 1950's.

526.

527.

528.

The majority of patriotic post cards sent to celebrate American holidays are those commemorating George Washington's birthday. Many of these show portraits of the first president, while many others depict scenes in the life of the man. Like other post cards, these date between 1900 and 1915.

529.

530.

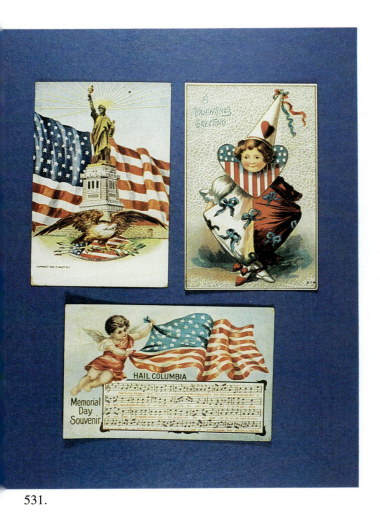

531.

532.

Other patriotic holidays celebrated in post cards include Veteran's Day and Memorial Day. One post card here (#531) is actually a Valentine, but it is so patriotic, it also covers Washington's and Lincoln's birthdays, both in February. This group of cards (#532) celebrates the 4th of July, and (#533) celebrate Lincoln's birthday.

533.

534.

535.

Saturday Evening Post covers are collectable works of art in their own right- but those that contain Halloween subject matter like this one (#534) from Oct. 1935, are especially so. The artwork is by Fredric Stanley.

Little Jack-o-lanterns like this 3 inch one (#535) with painted eyes were used as candy cups at Halloween parties in the 1940's & 1950's. It was made in the U.S.A.

HALLOWEEN

The golden days of October darken into haunted nights with flaming Jack-o-lanterns, black cats, and witches on broomsticks. Costumed children go "Trick or Treating" from door to door, and gather at parties to play games, the origins of which are long forgotten.

October 31st, Halloween, All Hallows Eve- even the name sends a shiver down our spines. Halloween is the second most collectable holiday after Christmas. In ancient times in Celtic countries, Halloween or Samhain (pronounced *Sowen*), marked the end of the old agricultural year. On this night, between the old year and the new, it is believed that the veil between the world of the living and that of the spirit is very thin, and departed loved ones can easily return.

In an almost universal tradition, lanterns were lit to guide the spirits of the deceased loved ones, and Jack-o-lanterns have been a part of the Halloween tradition ever since. They have been made of German pressed cardboard, composition, gauze, tin, plastic, and American papier mache. Originally, the facial features were all open to let the light shine out, but gradually they closed one by one as the Jack-o-lantern evolved into a candy container. There were other candy containers too, mostly made in Germany of cardboard, composition, or plaster. No other group of collectables, nor any other holiday, shows the creativity and the imagination that Halloween candy containers do. Many of these figures seem to be the spirits of vegetation, made of fruit and vegetable parts. Some are just "veggie people"- not made to contain candy.

There is also a great variety of noisemakers from early handmade wooden ratchets to tin clangers and rattles of the 1920's, 1930's, and 1940's.

Halloween parties are a tradition that echo the ancient gatherings and sacred rites, and for the do-it-yourselfer, there were party books to tell you just how to do it, from the Dennison "Bogie Books" of the 1910's to the 1930's to the "Weenie Witch" booklets of the 1950's.

As post cards go, Halloween post cards are rather uncommon and are a bit pricey, but they contain all the color, all the traditions, and all the imagination of more expensive Halloween collectables.

As the moon climbs high on this magical night and the witch mounts her broomstick for her midnight ride, light Jack-o-lantern, make a wish, and have a -

Happy Halloween!

536.

537-A.

Rare tin Jack-o-lanterns like this one (#536) were originally used as parade lanterns and carried on long poles. This one was made in the USA, about 1900. It is 6 1/2 inches in diameter. This little Jack-o-lantern (#537-A & #537-B) is a rare two-faced fellow. He was made in the USA, ca. 1940's and 1950's and is 6 inches high. Devils are actually very uncommon subjects for Halloween items. These (#538) are probably German. The tallest is 6 inches high and they date to the 1920's-1930's.

538.

537-B.

539.

This pumpkin head on a black cats body (#539) is rather unusual. It is American and dates to the 1930's-1940's. It is 7 inches tall. The tin Jack-o-lantern (#540-A & #540-B) is made by U.S. Metal Toy Co., who also produced many Halloween noisemakers. This one is missing the horn from its nose. It is 4 1/2 inches high and dates to the 1950's.

540-A.

540-B.

541.

542.

Here is a rare American devil head Jack-o-lantern (#541). It is made of papier mache and is 6 inches high and dates to the 1930's-1940's. These two owl Jack-o-lanterns (#542 & #544) are variations on the German pressed cardboard Jack-o-lantern. They are 4 1/2 inches high and date to the 1910's and 1920's. Two of these white skull lanterns (#543) are German and were made in the 1910's and 1920's. The one on the right is American, ca. 1930's, and is papier mache. The largest one is 5 inches high.

543.

544.

545.

This very rare devil on a skull Jack-o-lantern (#545) was made in Germany in the 1920's, and is 4 1/2 inches high. These two white Jack-o-lanterns (#546), sometimes called "ghosts", were made in Germany of pressed cardboard in the 1920's. The larger one is 6 1/2 inches.

546.

547.

548.

549.

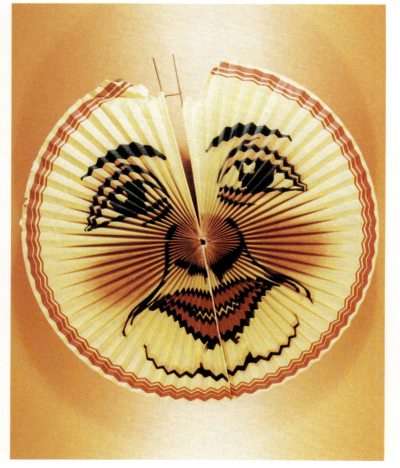

190

550.

551.

This rare gauze Jack-o-lantern (#547) must glow with a lit candle in it. It is about 7 inches high, and was probably made in Germany in the 1920's-1930's. The man in the moon paper lantern (#548) is 17 inches in diameter. It dates to the 1920's-1930's and is probably German. The orange paper lantern (#549) opens to about 1 foot high. It is Japanese and dates to the 1930's. Here are two devil head candy containers (#550 & 551). The first is German, made of composition, 3 inches high, and dates to the 1910's or 1920's. The second is also made in Germany. It is 3 1/2 inches high and dates to the 1930's-1940's. Below (#552) are two Jack-o-lanterns in transition. Not quite sure if they're lanterns or candy containers, their mouths are open but the eyes are closed and painted. They are American papier mache and date to the 1950's. The largest is 6 inches.

552.

553.

554.

Vegetable heads like this bisque pumpkin head (#553) or the composition figures below (#555) are among the most desirable of Halloween collectables. They are German and date to the 1920's and 1930's, the tallest of which is 4 inches. The beautiful owl (#554) is a German candy container. It is 3 1/2 inches high, ca. 1920's.

555.

556.

557.

The squash head (#556) is a candy container made of cardboard and composition. It is German, ca. 1920's and is 5 inches high. The little pumpkin head climbing a parsnip (#557) is also German composition, ca. 1910's-1920's and is 4 inches high. The three candy boxes below (#558) are all Japanese and date to the 1920's-1930's. The cardboard boxes are about 2 inches wide.

558.

560.

559.

561.

This is a very unusual egg crate witch (#559). It was made in the USA, ca. 1940's and is 9 inches tall. This whimsical little witch (#560) is of plaster and is a German candy container, ca. 1920's. She is 4 inches tall. Of the three candy containers below (#561) the center one is German, ca. 1920, and is 3 1/2 inches high. The other two are Japanese, ca. 1930's.

562.

This witch popping out of a pumpkin (#562) is one of the earliest we've seen. She is of composition, undoubtedly German, ca. 1900, and is 3 inches tall. This pressed cardboard witch (#563) is German and dates to the 1920's. She may be missing her broomstick. She is 9 inches to the top of her pointed hat. The two candy containers below (#564) with cardboard bodies were made in West Germany in the 1950's and are 7 inches high.

563.

564.

565.

566.

Here is a very unusual papier mache candy container in the form of a cat (#565). It seems to be recycled from a bunny mold. It is American, ca. 1940's, and is 7 inches high. This cat candy container (#566) is similar to one shown in our book *Halloween Collectables*, but it is uncommon in orange. It is American, ca. 1940's and is 7 inches high. The four little figures below (#567) seem to be wearing costumes from the Napoleonic War, and are seated on vegetables. They are 3 inches high and probably German made, ca. 1920's.

567.

568.

569.

This candy container, part carrot, part cat, (#568) is German, ca. 1930's. He is 5 1/2 inches high. The cat on this candy container (#569) is a squeaker. He is German, ca. 1920's and is 6 inches high. The cardboard cat hauling a cart (#570) and the tree stump next to it are by the Fibro-Toy Co., U.S.A. ca. 1940's. The cart is 8 1/2 inches in length.

570.

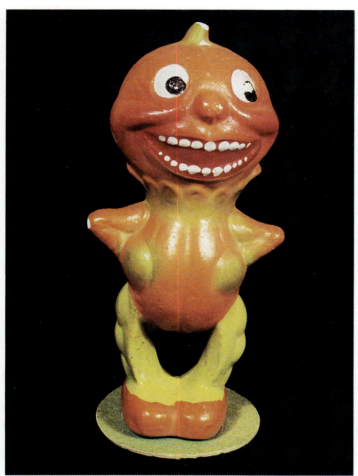
571.

572.

This bowlegged, bean-legged veggie man (#571) is German, ca. 1920's, and is 6 1/2 inches tall. These two witches (#572) are German candy containers and date to the 1920's and 1930's. The taller one is 6 1/2 inches high. The two plastic candy containers below (#573) are American, ca. 1940's-1950's, and are both 6 inches high.

573.

574.

575.

This glass pumpkin head man in a dust coat (#574) is a rare companion to the glass witch candy container shown in our *Halloween Collectables*. He is probably American, ca. 1900-1910's, and is 5 inches tall. These two German "nodders" made of wood and composition (#575), ca. 1920's, are each 7 inches tall. Of the two veggie people below (#576), one's head is on a spring and the other's ears are. They are probably German, ca. 1920's, and are 6 1/2 and 5 1/2 inches high.

576.

577.

578.

This little accordion squeaker (#577) was made in Germany in the 1910's-1920's and is 2 inches high. The cat blow-out (#578) is probably American ca. 1920's-1930's and the cat sticker in the center of the crepe paper rosette appears to be by Dennison. The two "frying pan" clangers below (#579) and the tin tambourine opposite (#582) are made by the J. Chein Co., makers of some of the most collectable tin toys, especially Halloween noisemakers.

579.

200

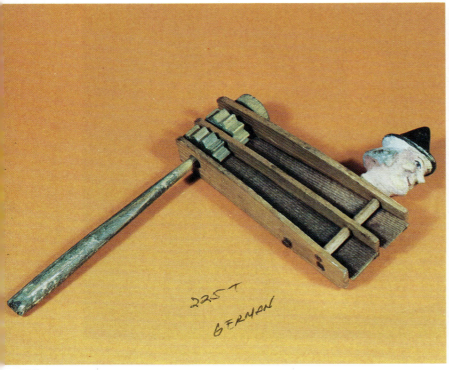

580.

581.

J. Chein began producing tin toys in the years prior to W.W. I in Harrison, NJ, and the Chein Co. is still in operation today, although they have been making only housewares since 1977. The toys they produced in the 1920's, 1930's, and 1940's are prized by collectors. The pieces shown here are from the 1920's and 1930's. The wooden ratchet noisemaker (#580) is a rare early German one, and is 7 inches high. The little candle squeaker (#581) is Japanese, ca. 1920's-1930's, and is 3 1/2 inches high.

582.

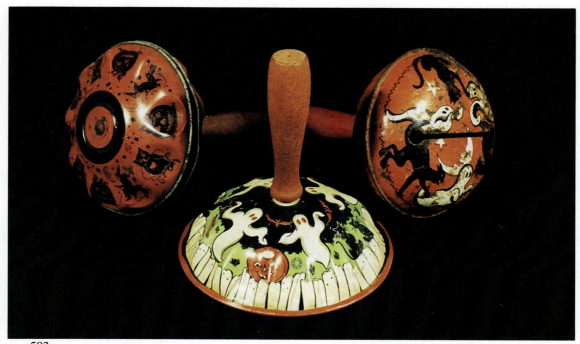

583.

Here are three noisemakers (#583) probably made by T. Cohn, U.S. Metal Toy Co., or Kirchhof, ca. 1930's. The egg crate devil's head is actually a horn (#584). It is American, ca. 1940's and 6 inches high, while the pipe (#585) is German, ca. 1920's and is 9 inches high. The cookie cutters (#586) in the 4 1/2 x 4 1/2 inch box are German, ca. 1930's and the candy molds (#587) are American, ca. 1910's-1920's. They are 3 inches square. The teapot and salt (#588) are part of a set shown in Halloween Collectables. They are German, ca. 1920's, and the teapot is 3 1/2 inches high.

584.

585.

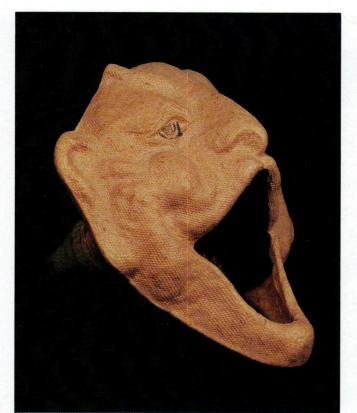

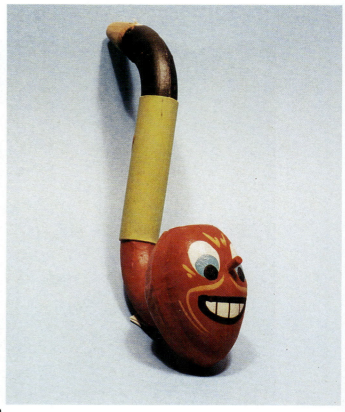

586.

587.

588.

203

589.

590.

The 6 inch high Steiff cat (#589) was made for Halloween in the 1950's. The springy witch (#590) is German, ca. 1920's-1930's. She is 11 inches tall. The two roly-poly witches below (#591) are of celluloid. They are 4 1/2 inches high, and are American, ca. 1920's.

591.

592.

593.

This wind-up toy (#592) was made in Japan by Durham Ind. Inc. in the 1950's. It is 6 inches tall and has metal gears. The little devil hand puppet (#593) is probably German, ca 1910's-1920's. It is 8 inches high. The cardboard and wood games pieces below (#594) are German, ca. 1920's-1930's and are 2 1/2 - 3 inches high.

594.

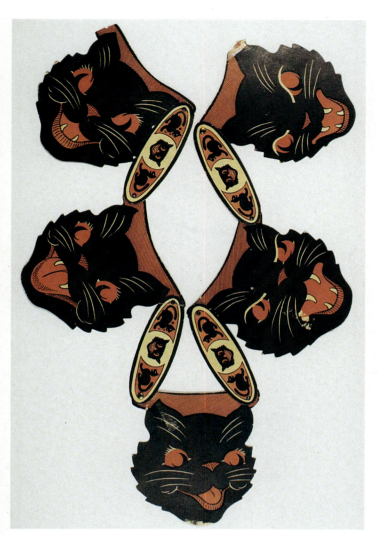

595.

596.

597.

206

598.

These two diecut cardboard festoons (#595 & #596) are eyeletted together to be folded. They are undoubtedly by Beistle, ca. 1910's-1930's. The honeycomb tissue garland (#597) is also possibly by Beistle, 1920's-1930's. The ghost (#598) with honeycomb "wings" is by Beistle, ca. 1910's-1930's, and is 11 inches high. The cardboard witch stirring her honeycomb cauldron (#599) is another Beistle creation, ca. 1926. It was made in three sizes from 6 to 10 1/2 inches in diameter.

599.

600.

601.

These two pressed cardboard tiaras (#600) are early German, ca. 1910's-1920's, and are exceptionally beautiful. The cat fan (#601) is also German. It is made of wood and tissue paper, ca. 1920's. All of the party hats on these pages were made by Beistle of cardboard and honeycomb tissue and date from 1925 (#602), 1928 (#603), and 1933 (#604 & #605).

602.

603.

604.

605.

209

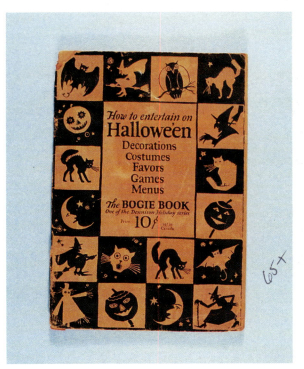

606.

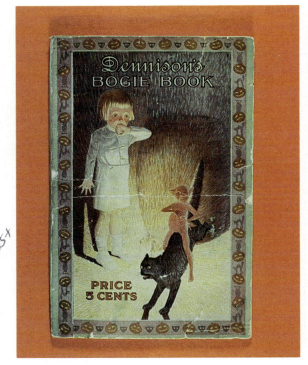

607.

Bogie Books like these (#606 & #607) are prized by collectors because of their own value, but they also help date other items. These were published by Dennison in 1916 and 1926 and are 5 x 7 inches. The "Halloween Suggestions" (#609), an 8 x 10 inch booklet, was published by Dennison in 1931 and replaced earlier Bogie Books. "Giving Dolly a Halloween Party" (#608), a paper doll, was printed in "The Delineator" for October 1912.

608.

609.

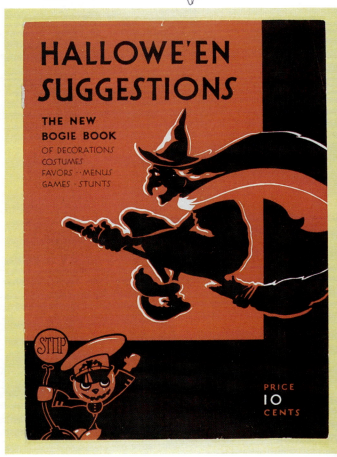

610.

The "Weeny Witch" booklets (#610) were produced by Essex Packers, a Canadian meat company, in the 1950's. They contain masks, games, and party suggestions for children. So do the October issues of *Play Mate* (#611 & #612). These magazines are popular for their artwork by Fern Bisel Peat.

611.   45+   612.   45+

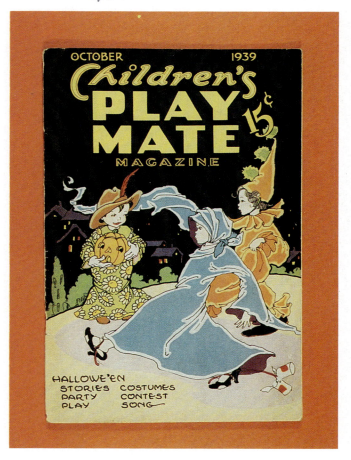

613.

As with all of the other holidays, Halloween post cards mostly date from between 1900 & 1915. The most popular topics are children, cats, and Jack-o-lanterns, but they also preserve for us some of our treasured Halloween traditions, such as bobbing for apples or mirror gazing (#617).

614.

615.

616.

One of the most popular publishers of Halloween post cards is, of course, Raphael Tuck (#614). Others are International Art Publishers, and John Winsch. Among the most sought after artists (#616) are B. Hoffman, Ellen Clappsaddle, and Frances Brundage. Post cards are among the most available and affordable Halloween collectables.

617.   618.

619.

620.

No collectables depict a holiday quite as perfectly as post cards. Like other holidays, most Thanksgiving post cards (#619) date from 1900-1915. This little turkey (#620) is a composition table decoration or party favor. It is probably Japanese, ca. 1940's-1950's, and is 3 1/2 inches high.

THANKSGIVING

The first Thanksgiving was celebrated in New England in 1621 by the pilgrims after they had harvested enough corn, barley, peas, and beans to see them through the coming Winter. Then, by a decree of Governor Bradford they held a Thanksgiving celebration that lasted three days. It was three days of feasting, games, and contests. Although Thanksgiving in its present form is a truly American holiday, in 1621 it was a carryover of the pagan harvest festival called *Lammas*, or *Lughnasad*.

In 1863, Abraham Lincoln declared the 4th Thursday of November to be a national day of Thanksgiving, and the holiday became one of more reverence than that celebrated in Plymouth, MA, in 1621. Today it is a day of family gatherings, food, and football, parades and pumpkin pies, and unless you begin the "holiday season" at Halloween like we do here at Flying Witch Farm, it is the beginning of the "holidays", the warmest, most wonderful time of the year.

The majority of Thanksgiving collectables are in the form of turkeys, once considered for the national emblem instead of the eagle. Wild turkeys were one of the many contributions to the first Thanksgiving dinner table by the native Americans and they are still a symbol of the holiday. There are turkey candy containers of composition, cardboard, and papier mache. There are candles that seem to be made in the same molds as the candy containers and there are turkeys both feathered and plucked and roasted.

To adorn the dinner table, there are centerpieces of cardboard and honeycomb tissue by the Beistle Co., and there are borders, table cloths, dinner napkins and nut cups by Dennison and C.A. Reed.

Post cards printed for the holiday feature turkeys, of course, but many also have an all American look about them, with flags and banners and Uncle Sam.

While the turkey is roasting in the oven and the bands are gathering on 34th Street, as the pies are cooling on the window sill and the cranberry jelly is being forgotten, enjoy the sounds and smells and the collectables of the holiday.

Happy Thanksgiving!

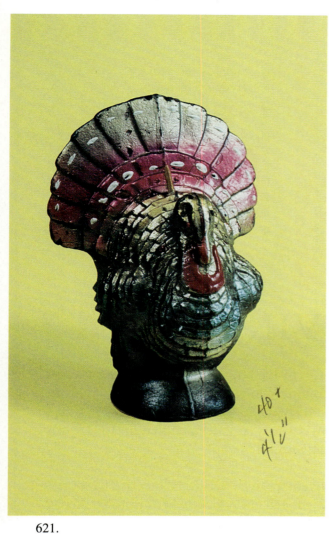

621.

622.

All of the turkeys on this page are candles made by the Gurley Candle Co. of Buffalo, NY in the 1950's. They appear to be replicas of the earlier German candy containers. These candles are handpainted in metallic colors typical of the 1950's. (#621 & #623) are large 4 1/2 inch candles, (#622) are both 3 inches.

623.

624.

The large turkey here (#625) is probably German, composition, and is a candy container that opens from below. It dates to the 1920's and is 4 1/2 inches high. (#624) is also a German candy container, ca. 1920's, but it has a removable head. It is 3 1/2 inches high. The "hen" candy container (#627) is probably German ca. 1930's and is 4 1/2 inches high. The smaller turkey (#626) is Japanese bisque, ca. 1930's-1940's, and is 2 inches high.

625.

626.

627.

#628

#629

The 3 inch turkey above (#628) is a German composition candy container, ca. 1920's-1930's. and the 3 1/2 inch turkey with spring legs on a box (#629) is a very unusual candy container. It is German, ca. 1930's. The two pilgrims, 5 1/2 inches high (#630), are candles by the Gurley Company. The tiny roasted turkey (#631) is a German pressed cardboard candy container, ca. 1910's-1920's and is 4 1/2 inches long. It opens from below.

The metal mold (#632) is for soap and is 3 1/2 inches long, while (#633) is a chocolate mold and is 4 inches long. The "egg crate" turkey (#634) is American. It was made by the Atco Company in the 1940's and is 7 inches high. The spectacular roast turkey candy container (#635) made of gesso over pressed cardboard, is German, ca. 1910's-1920's, and is a huge 9 1/2 inches long.

#630

#631

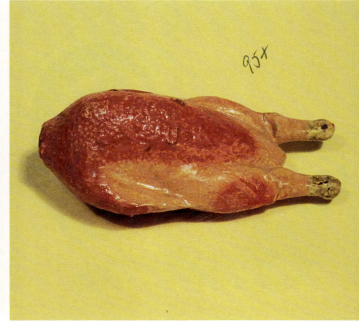

632.

633.

634.

635.

219

636.

637.

638.

220

639.

640.

The crepe paper borders (#636) are probably by Dennisons and date to the 1920's-1930's. The beautiful nut cups (#637) are of cardboard with tab and slot construction, while the crepe paper nut cups (#638) decorated with German scraps are probably by C.A. Reed, ca. 1940's.

The large cardboard diecut (#640) is 8 inches high and is probably by Beistle, ca. 1950's, while the small diecut (#639) is 2 1/2 inches high and possibly Dennisons, ca. 1920's-1930's. The printed cardboard turkey (#641) with the honeycomb tissue base is a Beistle centerpiece, ca. 1948, while the black honeycomb tissue turkey (#642) is also by Beistle, ca. 1939. Both are about 8 inches high.

641.

642.

PRICE GUIDE

To compile a price guide is to invite ridicule. There will always be the dealer who will say "Are they crazy? I wish I could buy it for that price!" While at the same time, another will say "I just bought that piece at a flea market for a tenth of that price!" Be that as it may, the prices given here are based on our own experiences in buying Holiday collectables in recent years. They do not reflect prices at garage sales or at specialized auctions. Naturally, price is dependent upon the condition of the piece as well as its scarcity. In the final analysis, a piece is only worth what you are willing to pay for it.

All of the photos in this book are numbered, from 1 to 642, and the number appears in this price guide in bold type. If there is more than one object in the photograph, then the prices given are from left to right.

1. ----
2. $75+
3. 45+
4. 35+
5. 45+
6. 35+
7. 35+
8. 25+
9. 45+
10. 45+
11. 150+
12. 45+
13. 35+
14. 35+
15. 100+
16. 125+
17. 25+
18. 30+
19. 125+
20. 95+
21. 95+
22. 65+
23. 45+
24. 35+
25. 25+
26. 25+
27. 125+
28. 125+
29. 95- 125+ ea.
30. 150+
31. 25+
32. 45+ ea.
33. 95+
34. 65+ ea.
35. 45+
36. 5+ ea. Santa
37. 5+ ea. Santa
38. 35+
39. 65+
40. 75+
41. 95+
42. 35+
43. 95+
44. 95+
45. 125+
46. 45+
47. 95+
48. 65+
49. 45+
50. 95+
51. 25+
52. 35+
53. 40+
54. 25+
55. 65+
56. 125+
57. 65+
58. 40+
59. 35+
60. 15+
61. 35+
62. 15+
63. 15+
64. 35+
65. 15+
66. 25+
67. 35+
68. 55+
69. 35+
70. 55+
71. 40+
72. 25+
73. 25+
74. 35+
75. 25+
76. 25+ ea.
77. 15+
78. 25+
79. 15+
80. 85+
81. 65+
82. 25+, 75+, 25+
83. 55+
84. 95+
85. 35 to 125+
86. 55+
87. 20+
88. 40+
89. 25 to 45+
90. 55+
91. 45+ ea.
92. 25+ ea.
93. 65+
94. 95+
95. 45+
96. 55+
97. 95+
98. 95+
99. 35+, 20+, 55+
100. 20 - 50+
101. 75+
102. 35+
103. 20 to 55+
104. 20 to 50+
105. 35+
106. 35+
107. 20 to 40+
108. 45+
109. 55+
110. 35+
111. 15+ ea.
112. 5+ ea.
113. 25+ ea.
114. 5 to 25+
115. 45+
116. 15+
117. 15+
118. 5 to 25+
119. 5 to 15+
120. 45+

#	Value	#	Value	#	Value
121.	25+ ea.	181.	5+ ea.	241.	400+
122.	small 5+, large 35+	182.	30+, 35+, 35+, 25+, 9+, 30+, 40+	242.	2,000+
123.	95+	183.	10+ ea.	243.	25+
124.	10+, 25+	184.	15+, 20+, 10+, 35+	244.	25+
125.	10+, 25+	185.	20+, 15+, 30+, 20+, 25+, 30+	245.	15+
126.	25+ ea.	186.	75+	246.	25+
127.	10+	187.	20+	247.	125+
128.	small 5+, large 35+	188.	35+	248.	35+
129.	20+ ea.	189.	45+ 6 ft.	249.	75+
130.	5-35+	190.	15+	250.	45+
131.	45+	191.	5+ per section	251.	45+
132.	15+	192.	45+ ea. large, 25+ ea. small	252.	35+
133.	25+	193.	15+ ea.	253.	25+
134.	35+, 25+	194.	15+ ea.	254.	25+
135.	35+ ea.	195.	10+ ea.	255.	75+
136.	45+ ea.	196.	45-65+ ea.	256.	150+
137.	35+	197.	45+ bench w/ 2 figures	257.	125+
138.	15-25+ ea.	198.	25+ ea.	258.	500+
139.	15-25+ ea.	199.	65+ all together	259.	85+
140.	5-15+ ea.	200.	20+ ea.	260.	65+
141.	10+	201.	45+	261.	900+
142.	10 -15+	202.	10-15+ ea.	262.	2,500+
143.	5-15+ ea.	203.	20+	263.	1,200+
144.	10+ ea.	204.	10+ ea.	264.	250+
145.	35+	205.	45+	265.	65+
146.	30+	206.	10-15+ ea.	266.	10-30+ ea. (w/o cookies)
147.	10+	207.	10-25+ ea.	267.	5+
148.	25+ the box	208.	15-20+ ea.	268.	5-35+
149.	3-5+ ea.	209.	20+	269.	165+, 125+, 100+
150.	5+	210.	5+	270.	10+
151.	250+ (rare)	211.	15-20+ ea.	271.	10+ ea.
152.	5+	212.	20+	272.	10+ ea.
153.	25+ ea.	213.	25+ ea.	273.	10+
154.	2 to 5+	214.	25+, 35+	274.	10+
155.	15+	215.	10+ ea.	275.	5+ ea.
156.	15+	216.	5+ ea.	276.	295+
157.	75¢ ea.	217.	35+ ea.	277.	125+ ea.
158.	10+	218.	5+	278.	65+, 55+
159.	10+	219.	25-35+ ea.	279.	450+
160.	10+ ea.	220.	15+	280.	125+
161.	1+ ea., 15+ box	221.	8+ ea.	281.	295+, 350+, 250+
162.	1+ ea.	222.	3-25+ ea.	282.	325+ ea.
163.	10+ pkg.	223.	10+	283.	650+
164.	3+ per ft., 5+ per ft.	224.	55+	284.	195+ ea.
165.	10+	225.	3-25+ ea.	285.	850+
166.	3+ ea.	226.	150+	286.	95-175+
167.	25+	227.	25+	287.	600-1,200+
168.	3+ ea.	228.	85+	288.	3,500+
169.	3+ ea.	229.	15+	289.	850+
170.	35+	230.	15+	290.	2,500+ (A&B together)
171.	35+ ea.(w/ lights)	231.	15+	291.	150+
172.	75+ (w/ lights)	232.	15+	292.	150+
173.	60+ (w/ lights)	233.	15+	293.	2,500+
174.	15+ (w/ lights)	234.	15+	294.	2,000+
175.	10+ (w/ lights)	235.	45+	295.	750+
176.	3+ ea.	236.	10-20+ ea.	296.	900+
177.	25+ box, 50+ (w/ lights)	237.	10-20+ ea.	297.	7,500+
178.	10+	238.	10-20+ ea.	298.	750+ ea.
179.	35+	239.	10-20+ ea.	299.	2,500+
180.	10+, 20+, 10+, 10+, 10+	240.	10-20+ ea.	300.	1,500+

301.	950+	361.	45+	421.	5+
302.	3,000+	362.	20+	422.	95+
303.	1,500+	363.	20+	423.	65+
304.	1,250+	364.	15+ ea.	424.	195+
305.	350+	365.	65+	425.	55+
306.	300+	366.	175+	426.	45+
307.	125+ ea.	367.	55+	427.	45+
308.	65+	368.	55+	428.	45+
309.	350+	369.	55+	429.	25+ ea.
310.	125+	370.	55+	430.	55+
311.	20+	371.	45+	431.	25+
312.	20+	372.	45+	432.	65+
313.	20+	373.	125+	433.	45+
314.	10+	374.	5-10+ ea.	434.	25+, 30+, 25+
315.	10+	375.	10+	435.	45+
316.	15+	376.	5-10+ ea.	436.	25-65+
317.	55+ (w/ box)	377.	5-10+ ea.	437.	95+
318.	15-35+ ea.	378.	5-10+ ea.	438.	125+
319.	25+	379.	5-10+ ea.	439.	125+
320.	10+ ea.	380.	10+	440.	125+
321.	45+	381.	10+	441.	65+, 45+
322.	35+	382.	10+	442.	225+
323.	5+ ea.	383.	15+	443.	150+, 250+, 150+
324.	5+ ea.	384.	10+	444.	250+
325.	5-10+ ea.	385.	10+	445.	175+
326.	5-10+ ea.	386.	25+	446.	250+, 200+
327.	5-10+ ea.	387.	25+	447.	300+, 225+, 150+
328.	5-10+ ea.	388.	25+	448.	300+
329.	5-10+ ea.	389.	25+	449.	250+
330.	5-10+ ea.	390.	45+ for booklet	450.	350+
331.	125+ (w/ frame)	391.	125+	451.	150+
332.	50+	392.	15+	452.	175+
333.	95+	393.	10+	453.	125+
334.	75+	394.	15+	454.	95+
335.	95+	395.	15+ ea.	455.	25+
336.	125+	396.	25+	456.	125+
337.	65+	397.	25+	457.	125+
338.	55+	398.	35+	458.	425+
339.	45+	399.	95+	459.	350+
340.	45+	400.	65+ pair	460.	550+
341.	45+	401.	150+	461.	175+
342.	45+	402.	175+	462.	175+
343.	45+	403.	225+	463.	90-225+
344.	45+	404.	95+	464.	5+ per chick
345.	35+ ea.	405.	55+	465.	35+
346.	35+	406.	95+, 95+, 75+	466.	5+ ea.
347.	35+	407.	20+	467.	8+ ea.
348.	35+	408.	95+, 125+, 95+	468.	95+
349.	65+	409.	10+	469.	175+
350.	15+	410.	5+	470.	35+ ea.
351.	10+	411.	10+ ea.	471.	50+
352.	10+	412.	5+ ea.	472.	95+, 125+
353.	10+	413.	10+ ea.	473.	175+
354.	65+	414.	10+ ea.	474.	175+ all
355.	65+	415.	5+ ea.	475.	350+
356.	45+, 65+, 35+	416.	95+ (basket only)	476.	35+ ea.
357.	55+	417.	15+	477.	75+
358.	55+	418.	15+	478.	225+
359.	45+	419.	45+	479.	45+
360.	45+	420.	5+	480.	35+

481.	25+	541.	400+	601.	65+
482.	35+	542.	325+	602.	95+
483.	45+	543.	350+, 250+, 350+	603.	95+
484.	225+	544.	325+	604.	45+ ea.
485.	75+	545.	450+	605.	95+
486.	45+	546.	300+, 400+	606.	65+
487.	55+	547.	325+	607.	65+
488.	75+	548.	125+	608.	25+
489.	75+	549.	65+	609.	65+
490.	10+ ea.	550.	275+	610.	10+ ea.
491.	15+	551.	250+	611.	45+
492.	15+ ea.	552.	85+ ea.	612.	45+
493.	15+	553.	125+	613.	15-25+ ea.
494.	10-15+ ea.	554.	175+	614.	15-25+ ea.
495.	5-10+ ea.	555.	125+, 125+, 150+, 125+	615.	15-25+ ea.
496.	65+	556.	275+	616.	15-25+ ea.
497.	45+	557.	425+	617.	15-25+ ea.
498.	3+ ea.	558.	125+ ea.	618.	15-25+ ea.
499.	125+	559.	325+	619.	5-10+ ea.
500.	65+, 45+, 15+	560.	275+	620.	45+
501.	325+	561.	125+, 150+, 125+	621.	40+
502.	250+ ea.	562.	250+	622.	25+ ea.
503.	325+	563.	325+	623.	40+ ea.
504.	150+, 35+, 95+	564.	75+ ea.	624.	125+
505.	225+	565.	275+	625.	175+
506.	225+	566.	275+	626.	55+, 75+
507.	400+	567.	300+ ea.	627.	65+
508.	85+	568.	225+	628.	125+
509.	35+	569.	275+	629.	125+
510.	25+	570.	150+, 35+	630.	10+ ea.
511.	75+	571.	350+	631.	95+
512.	500+	572.	275+, 375+	632.	35+
513.	25+	573.	75+ ea.	633.	35+
514.	35+	574.	500+	634.	75+
515.	15+	575.	475+ ea.	635.	165+
516.	15+ ea.	576.	525+ ea.	636.	$1 per ft
517.	25+	577.	225+	637.	8+ ea.
518.	15+	578.	65+	638.	15+ ea.
519.	125+	579.	95+, 65+	639.	8+
520.	25+, 35+	580.	225+	640.	12+
521.	10+ ea.	581.	95+	641.	45+
522.	45+ the booklet	582.	65+	642.	45+
523.	65+, 45+	583.	35+, 40+, 35+		
524.	10+	584.	325+		
525.	5+	585.	325+		
526.	15+	586.	125+		
527.	10+	587.	65+ ea.		
528.	10-15+ ea.	588.	250+ all		
529.	10-15+ ea.	589.	75+		
530.	10-15+ ea.	590.	225+		
531.	10-15+ ea.	591.	250+ ea.		
532.	10-15+ ea.	592.	325+		
533.	10-15+ ea.	593.	250+		
534.	15+	594.	25+ ea.		
535.	30+	595.	65+		
536.	750+	596.	65+		
537.	250+	597.	25+		
538.	500+ ea.	598.	55+		
539.	325+	599.	95+		
540.	50+	600.	150+ ea.		

ACKNOWLEDGMENTS

All of the collectables shown in this book are from the collection at Flying Witch Farm, with the exception of those in the following photographs, for which we gratefully acknowledge:

Julia Bartels; 163, 220, 226, 242, 247, 249, 255, 256, 257, 258, 261, 263, 264, 269, 277, 279, 281-292, 323, 324, 356, 359, 360, 361, 367, 376, 378, 379, 395, 417, 432-434, 476, 508, 511, 513, 515, 521, 523, 524, 536, 547-550, 561, 564, 577, 588, 593, 597, 608, 612.

Charles Gottschall; 175, 177, 182, 241, 395, 402, 407, 409, 422, 424, 512, 526, 592, 636.

Sharon & Joe Happle; 391, 401, 403, 406, 408, 419, 458, 459, 460, 463, 502, 507, 538, 542, 545, 572, 574, 576, 591.

Rosemary Johnson; 254.

Pat Patruccio; 552, 554, 589.

Gail & Jay Reuben; 197-200, 219.

Francine Schmitt; 19, 20, 21, 22, 322, 332, 393, 396, 411, 420, 421, 436, 443-453, 470-472, 484, 517, 518, 629, 633-635.

Dolores & Pete Thompson; 541, 543, 544, 546, 551, 559, 566-568, 571, 575, 584, 585, 590.

All photos by Dan Campanelli.